Traditional KNITTING

Patterns of
Ireland, Scotland and
England

Traditional KNITTING

Patterns of
Ireland, Scotland and England

GWYN MORGAN

St. Martin's Press
New York.

Acknowledgments

The publisher and author gratefully acknowledge the help of Gillian Green, who edited the patterns in this book. Our thanks also go to Stella Clifford, Sylvia Morgan and Wendy Page who helped with the knitting of the patterns, and to Tom Miles for technical advice.

We would also like to thank the following for kindly providing photographs:

British Tourist Authority page 18; Royal Danish Ministry for Foreign Affairs page 76; Geoff Goode pages 53 and 97; Hamburg Kunsthalle page 9; Irish Tourist Board page 59; National Trust for Scotland pages 13 and 75; Shetland Museum and Library page 14; Victoria and Albert Museum pages 8 and 10.

All other photographs were taken by Michael Busselle.

Contents

Introduction

Knitting is a simple craft and the basic skill is easily acquired. It is estimated that at the present time six million people in Britain alone possess it. In recent years interest in knitting has increased dramatically, promoted by the growing popularity of craftwork and by commercial fashion designers, much of whose inspiration is drawn from the rich traditional heritage.

The British Isles have produced some of the finest craft knitting in the world, principally among the fishing communities of Ireland, the northern isles of Scotland and the east coast of England. But this tradition need not die with its originators; the beauty of Aran, Fair Isle and Guernsey designs is timeless.

This book does not provide a simple introduction to knitting; many others exist to fulfil that need. Neither is it an exhaustive study of traditional knitting. Its aim is to encourage those who wish to progress beyond the simple knitting pattern, to be more ambitious and creative in their craft.

Aran and Fair Isle garments are never out of fashion, yet prices have soared recently and the quality is often low. The true Guernsey was almost an endangered species, but in the last few years it has enjoyed a revival in popularity. This book aims to explain the essentials of these regional traditions and to show the infinite variety that can be developed within them.

Traditional knitting patterns have in the past been handed down by word of mouth and printed patterns particularly for Guernseys are not easy to find. It is hoped that the patterns published here will help knitters to discover the satisfaction that can be gained from producing these high-quality and beautiful garments.

1
An Ancient Craft

Exactly how and when the craft of knitting developed in Europe is uncertain. While there is plenty of proof that textile production in wool and flax was important from prehistoric times, the products were either woven or made using the twined-warp technique known as sprang.

To find the earliest evidence of knitting, we have to turn to Egypt. We know that around AD 400 members of the Christian sect known as the Copts were producing knitted sandal socks, bags and dolls. Their exact method of knitting is unknown. A frame may have been used, but a single needle or pair of needles is also possible. Whatever the technique, the result was a fabric made in a crossed stocking stitch.

It is usually suggested that knitting was brought to Europe in the eighth century by the Arabs who conquered North Africa and then Spain. On the other hand, Coptic Christians were influential in Northern Europe before this. The earliest monasteries in the British Isles took many of their ideas from the monks of the Egyptian desert. A seventh century poem describes the Welsh monastery of Bangor as a:

> *House full of delight*
> *Built on the rock*
> *And indeed true vine*
> *Transplanted from Egypt.*

Coptic elements are also found in the design of Irish ecclesiastical manuscripts and carved stone slabs, while pottery from the eastern Mediterranean occurs on many sixth century sites in Ireland and western Britain. It is not impossible that Coptic craftsmen and refugees fled before the Muslim armies to Ireland, which at this time was one of the great centres of Christian culture. But until fragile and elusive fragments of textiles are excavated we can only speculate about the early development of knitting.

For the next thousand years the craft of knitting rarely surfaces from almost total obscurity. Such everyday activities hardly ever make the history books. A rare exception is Marco Polo's account in 1272 of the monks of Barsarno in Persia who knitted woollen girdles which were reputed to have healing powers. Evidently the craft was alive and well in the Middle Ages, for fragments of knitted material have turned up on the excavations of thirteenth to fifteenth century sites in countries as far apart as Russia, Poland, France and Spain.

A pair of red wool knitted socks (4th–5th century)

The Church probably fostered the highest standards of medieval craftsmanship. Pope Innocent IV was said to have been buried in 1254 wearing a pair of knitted altar gloves and the bishop who was interred in the fourteenth century tomb at the cathedral church of Ross was similarly attired.

The most vivid illustration of medieval knitting is the painting executed by Master Bertram about 1400 on the panel of the Buxtehude altarpiece entitled *The Visit of the Angels*. Here the Virgin Mary is shown passing her time usefully by completing a vest on four needles, while balls of wool sit tidily in a basket by her side.

In the late fifteenth century knitwear production emerges as a flourishing industry. At the luxury end of the market were superb gloves, a Spanish speciality, finely made in silk and gilt thread. France had built up a reputation for silk and worsted stockings, England for knitted caps. In 1488 Henry VII tried to fix the price of British woollens; that of 'knytted woollen caps' to two shillings.

These hats remained in fashion for over a century. They regularly appear in the portrait gallery of Tudor characters painted by Hans Holbein. In 1571 an attempt

The Visit of the Angels *(c. 1400) shows the Virgin Mary knitting*

was made to stimulate trade with the 'Cappers' Act', which laid down that every person above the age of six years (except 'maids, ladies, gentlewomen, noble personages, and every lord, knight and gentleman of 20 marks' land'), residing in any of the cities, towns, villages or hamlets of England, should wear on Sundays and

9

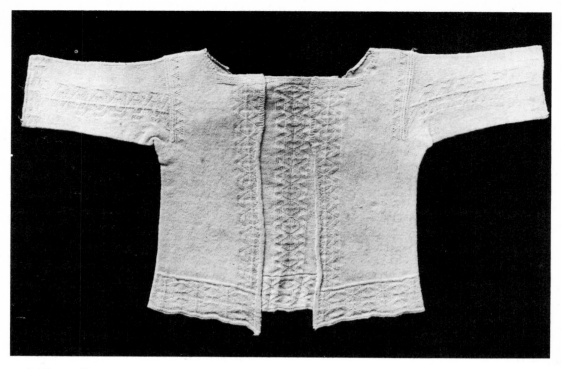

A child's woollen knitted vest (English, 17th century)

holidays (except when travelling), 'a cap of wool, thicked and dressed in England, made within this realm, and only dressed and finished by some of the trade of cappers, upon pain to forfeit for every day of not wearing 3s 4d.'.

The sixteenth century was the high point of the European hand-knitting industry. On the Continent professional knitting guilds flourished, whose apprentices served for seven years before qualifying. At the end of that time the apprentice had to produce within 13 weeks a bonnet, a pair of gloves, a woollen jacket and an elaborately patterned carpet.

In England, the important centres of production were Yorkshire, Norfolk, Leicester, Nottingham and London. Philip Stubbs in *The Anatomy of Abuses* (1583) complained at the excessive expenditure of far from wealthy people on knitted silk stockings when 'the price of these be a Royal, or twentie shillings, as commonly it is. For how can it be less when the very knitting is worth a noble or a Royal or much more?'.

In 1589 the death blow was dealt to the hand-knitting industry: William Lee of Nottinghamshire invented the knitting frame. The machine was relatively slow to catch on; Queen Elizabeth I refused it a patent on the grounds that it would damage the existing industry and Lee later died in obscurity.

Nevertheless within a century the new knitting frame had taken over. Hand knitting persisted in the remoter parts of Britain. In the Yorkshire Dales until the nineteenth century men and women alike knitted stockings as they walked about, which sold for £2 a pair. Both Daniel Defoe and Arther Young refer to hand knitting in several areas of the British Isles, and in 1805 the annual export of hand-knitted woollen stockings from Aberdeen was valued at £100,000. The spread of the railways dealt the final blow to these last outposts of commercial hand knitting.

Only in the coastal villages of eastern England, Scotland and Ireland did the local traditions in hand knitting continue. The Guernseys, Fair Isles and Arans were part of the fishing communities' own folk culture and not their economic mainstay, hence proved more resistant to technological change.

Elsewhere in Britain knitting continued as a popular domestic craft, a suitable pastime for ladies with a considerable amount of time on their hands. The 1840s and 1850s saw the appearance of the first published knitting patterns such as Mrs Gaugain's *Little Knitting, Netting and Crochet Book*. While she promoted many beautiful traditional patterns, most of her contemporaries concentrated on a welter of knick-knacks and such 'useful' items as tea cosies, pen wipers, bell pulls and egg warmers.

The Crimean War encouraged a more practical response on the home front, resulting in the patriotic production of knitted balaclavas and warm clothing. The turn of the century saw a growing reaction against the fussiness of Victorian taste, reflected in the women's magazines of the period. The changing role of women, the increasing popularity of outdoor activities such as cycling and tennis and the tendency to less restrictive clothing affected the type of knitwear that was produced. This was when the sports' sweater or jumper made its first appearance.

Something of a minor social revolution was the appearance in 1899 of John Paton Son & Co's *Universal Knitting Book*, price one penny. This marked the entry of the manufacturers of knitting wool into the business of promoting domestic knitting through their own patterns. Patons were rapidly followed by the firm of J & J Baldwin & Partners with its publication *Woolcraft*, which soon became a household word.

The years after the Second World War witnessed the continuing popularity of knitting, with the emphasis very much on the practical approach: straightforward if unexciting designs particularly for children, the ubiquitous pullover, easily washable man-made fibres, and thicker, quick-knit yarns.

The last decade has heralded a revival of interest in traditional crafts, natural materials and knitwear as high fashion. Individual craft knitters like Kaffe Fassett and Sasha Kagan have extended the art, experimenting with new materials and colours, but keeping a healthy respect for traditional designs. In fact, knitwear has emerged from the doldrums into something of a renaissance.

2
From Sheep to Yarn

Sheep were among the earliest animals to be domesticated. As well as producing meat, milk and manure they supply what has always been a major textile fibre – wool. Wool is water repellent and also warm due to the natural crimp of the wool fibre which traps air and gives good insulation. The crimp of the fibres also allows them to lock together easily when spun and so to form a stable yarn.

Once a sheep has been sheared the wool within the fleece must be sorted. The different qualities of wool within the fleece vary according to the breed of sheep and its living conditions. The fibre length, strength, softness and colour and the amount of coarse hair (kemp) are all important factors. The wool from the shoulders of the animal will be of the highest quality, that from the rest of the back will be second best, while that from the belly and legs will be coarser and contain a proportion of kemp.

Wool acquires a large variety of impurities while on a sheep's back – natural secretions of grease and dung, burrs, twigs and sand and also branding agents applied by the shepherd such as paint and tar. These must all be removed by scouring the fleece before further work can be carried out.

Knots and tangles are removed from the wool in a final process before spinning. The way this is achieved depends on the type of yarn – wool for soft, thick, 'woollen' yarns is carded, then spun from the shorter fibres of the fleece, while the longer, finer fibres used in worsted yarns are combed before being spun.

Carding has been carried out since the Middle Ages on a pair of small square boards or 'cards' set with metal hooks and held with handles. A handful of wool is placed on the hooks of one card and the other card is repeatedly stroked across in one direction. This draws the wool out flat with the fibres all lying in the same direction. Then, by reversing the stroke of the card, the wool is rolled into a long sausage which is then ready for spinning. The yarn is then spun at right angles to the direction in which the fibres lie.

The wool for worsted yarn is combed out using special heated combs so that the fibres lie parallel to one another in a roving. This is then spun parallel to the direction in which the fibres lie to produce a much finer yarn than the soft woollen. Worsteds are generally used for woven fabrics, and woollens for soft knitting wools. However fishermen's Guernseys, which are made to be extremely tough and hard wearing, are knitted in a worsted yarn.

The traditional method of shearing, the first stage in producing yarns, is still used on Fair Isle

The process of spinning is very simple – the fibres are twisted together while under tension. The simplest way to achieve this is to use a spindle, weighted at one end, to which the wool is attached. By twisting the spindle and letting it drop the wool fibre will be spun together and a stable yarn formed. The disadvantage of this method is that once the spindle has reached the ground the process must stop while the spun yarn is wound on and the process is then repeated. However it can be done virtually anywhere, and hand spinners can still be seen in the fields in the Middle East and Southern Europe.

The first continuous spinning device was recorded by Leonardo da Vinci in 1519, and by the mid sixteenth century spinning wheels which allowed the process of twisting and winding to take place simultaneously were in use throughout Europe, greatly increasing the output of the spinster. This system whereby one spinster produced one thread was still in use at the beginning of the eighteenth century. But with the invention of the spinning jenny and the mule towards the end of the

From fleece to yarn – carding, spinning and knitting, as carried out by a Shetland family

century, the process became highly automated. The mechanisation of spinning is now so sophisticated that a wide variety of yarns can be produced.

The final knitting yarn is made by twisting several strands together. The ply of the wool refers to the number of strands, but the character of the wool depends on the thickness of the individual strands and the amount of twist put into them; increasing the amount of twist will increase the strength and durability of the yarn.

Man-made fibre manufacture produces yarn in the same way that a silkworm spins. These continuous filament yarns are strong and uniform but lack the character of wool. The early man-made yarns were too smooth to be used as a substitute for wool, but with the bulking and texturising of continuous filament synthetics they have increasingly replaced wool in mass-produced knitting yarns. Synthetic fibres have some advantages such as easy washing and cheapness, but they never achieve the natural texture and warmth of pure wool.

3
The Knitting Process

Knitting is the production of a fabric by the interlinking of a continuous thread. A row of loops is set on to a needle and a series of stitches interlocking one above the other is formed as the fabric is built up. Each new stitch as it is formed secures the one beneath, and the loop of the old stitch is left either at the back or front of the new one. This is the difference between a knit and a purl stitch; a knit stitch leaves the loop at the back of the fabric, while a purl stitch leaves the loop at the front. If a stitch is not secured but simply 'dropped' the interlinking stitches will undo in a vertical line or 'ladder'.

Stocking stitch is obtained if all the loops are left at the back of the fabric. This is produced by working in knit stitch on the right side of the fabric and in purl stitch on the wrong side of the fabric. By using combinations of knit and purl stitches a wide variety of textures can be formed and patterns built up. Moving groups of stitches to the back or front of other groups of stitches produces a cabled effect.

Generally garments are made in separate pieces, working backwards and forwards (that is from right side to wrong side) with a pair of needles. However, some garments such as gloves and socks and also some Guernseys are better made without seams. This means producing a tube of knitted fabric by knitting in the round.

Knitting in the round requires a set of four or more needles, pointed at both ends, or a circular needle, and the knitting is carried on continuously in the same direction. By always using a knit stitch the loops are always to the back of the fabric and stocking stitch is the result. Knitwear produced in this way is tougher and can be harder wearing than that with seams.

Any pattern given with a back and front can be worked in the round by adding the number of stitches for front and back together and casting on with 4 needles or a circular needle. The body is then made as a tube to under the arms where front and back must be split and knitted separately, working backwards and forwards on a pair of needles.

To produce a garment from any pattern, the most important step is first to check your tension. This boring procedure, known as knitting a tension square, is vital to the success of a garment. As long as the tension matches the tension stated in the pattern, any comparable yarn can be substituted for the yarn specified. However good you may think your knitting is, the tension you produce may not be the same as that of the pattern designers. Failure to check can result in some miserable disasters – there is nothing worse than spending a lot of time and effort on knitting something that ends up two sizes too large.

This can be avoided by knitting a tension square about 10cm/4 inches square so that you can measure a 5cm/2 inch square without distortion. If the tension varies from that stated, you must try again with another needle size – smaller if you have too few stitches and larger if you have too many. When your tension matches that stated in the pattern you can start on the interesting work by following the pattern.

It is a good idea to check that the measurements stated in the pattern are the measurements you want to fit into. Garments can be altered to fit any size by working an extra number of stitches per inch according to the tension measurement, or fewer as needed. Alternatively, more rows, or fewer can be worked to vary the lengths given.

Complicated designs in knitting are easiest to follow from charts. The design is drawn out in detail on graph paper where each small square represents a stitch, with each row of squares representing a row in the knitting. This then shows the form of the design and allows the knitting to be checked for mistakes much more easily than when following written instructions. On the other hand, Aran patterns are written out in full rather than being shown in chart form. Aran designs use travelling stitches, particularly to produce cable effects, which cannot be easily conveyed in charts.

If a garment is being knitted in the round from a chart the knitter starts at the bottom right hand corner of the chart and works from right to left for each round. If a garment is being knitted on two needles the knitter again starts at the bottom right hand corner of the chart and works from right to left for the first and all right side rows, but back from left to right for the second and all wrong side rows.

Charts are used in this book both for Guernsey patterns – showing knit and purl stitches – and for all colour knitting. Charts showing knit and purl stitches require some thought in their use. The representations for knit and purl remain constant if knitting in the round as the knitting is always carried out from the right side. However, if knitting on two needles the representations for knit and purl on right side rows must be reversed when knitting a wrong side row. Although this sounds complicated in theory it is quite simple to follow in practice.

Colour charts are self explanatory, the knitting being worked in stocking stitch throughout. All the traditional patterns given here use only two colours in any one row. While any one colour is in use, the other must be carried across the back of the fabric until it is needed again. If the gaps to be bridged are less than five stitches the yarn can be stranded, that is, left loosely at the back of the work taking care not to pull this strand too tight.

For a neat and firmer finish or for wider gaps, the yarn is woven across the fabric. This involves catching the yarn behind every alternate stitch as it is worked by passing it over the colour in use when knitting one stitch and under the colour in use when knitting the next.

4
Guernseys

Guernseys (or ganseys) are the traditional upper garments worn by fishermen, designed to be warm and waterproof. The name derives from the Channel Island where a type of Guernsey is still knitted, though most of these are now machine-made. Guernseys also survive in fishing communities along the east coast of England, from Suffolk, through Norfolk and Lincolnshire, Yorkshire and Northumberland, to Scotland and her islands. But with the decline of inshore fishing, vastly improved communications and the availability of cheap, machine-made substitutes, this rich tradition has almost died out.

The different areas show broad regional variations, but even within these, each close-knit community tended to develop distinctive patterns of its own. Individual families would often keep the same patterns for their garments, handing them down for generations. The designs and symbols used in the stitch patterns reflected their way of life by the sea.

Gladys Thompson in *Patterns for Guernseys, Jerseys and Arans* lists 21 basic patterns including cable or rope stitch, anchor, herringbone, flag, triple wave, tree of life, single zig-zag or lightning and double zig-zag, known in Scotland as 'marriage lines' or 'ups and downs'.

Many patterns indicate the nets of the fishermen. The east coast of England was settled by Vikings from the ninth century AD and Old Norse words still survive in the local dialect and place-names. The Flamborough pattern 'net mask', for example, incorporates the Norse word 'mask' meaning stitch.

The fishermen worked on the land as well as the sea, and their farming activities are represented by the pattern known as 'ridge and furrow', indicating the corrugated effect of ploughed earth. The basic design of the Guernsey is made up of vertical panels in which purl stitches form the pattern on a background of plain, separated by cables and areas of 'sand and shingle' (for example single or double moss).

In England, Guernseys are traditionally knitted in a tightly spun 4 or 5 ply worsted, usually dark blue in colour, on fine needles, to produce a firm fabric which is not only windproof but will also 'turn water'. In Scotland a softer spun, black wool is generally preferred.

The construction of the traditional Guernsey is unique: the garment is knitted in one piece so that the structural weakness of seams is eliminated. The shape is essentially square and it is designed to be fairly close fitting, with gussets under the arms to allow freedom of movement. The shoulders are usually grafted together;

A Guernsey, as worn by a crab fisherman

and the sleeves, generally knitted from shoulder to cuff, are always made fairly short so as not to get in the way of the fisherman.

At the start of the work many fisherwives would cast on in double wool and also cast off the cuffs in the same way. This gives a very firm finish to the edges of the Guernsey where the wear is greatest.

Five 45cm/18 inch steel needles were always used in Yorkshire, while further north a greater number of shorter ones was used. The static needle holding the work was held by a knitting sheath, which provided a support for the weight of the work and allowed the knitting to work more easily. A shaft of wood about 15cm/6 inches long had a hole in one end in which the needle was placed, and it was kept in position on the right of the knitter by being tucked into the waistband. In Scotland a leather pouch attached to a belt was used. Sets of needles suitable for this work are difficult to obtain now, but a circular needle can be used instead.

The garment is worked in the round up to under the arms; seam stitches (single stitches worked contrary to the main pattern) are used to mark the side 'seam', starting at the top of the welt. Some knitters used to work the initials of the wearer above the welt. Gussets are worked by increasing in the centre of the seam stitches and are continued into the sleeve.

Just under the arms the back and front are split and knitted separately to form the yoke. The yoke is normally the patterned area of the Guernsey, although some, like the Channel Island Guernsey, are plain throughout, while others, particularly those worn for 'best', may be patterned throughout.

At the top of the yoke the back and front are generally grafted together on the shoulder, sometimes with a shoulder extension incorporated between the two. The neck stitches are picked up on four needles and the ribbed neckband is worked in the round. In Scotland a tighter finish is sometimes achieved by making an open neckband which is fastened by buttons.

In most Guernseys, the sleeve stitches are picked up round the armhole and the sleeve worked downwards on four needles, decreasing to the cuff. This means that the sleeves can be repaired by pulling back from the cuff and reknitting. Perhaps for this reason the sleeves are usually plain, any decoration being restricted to the top.

The instructions for knitting Guernseys used to be handed down from mother to daughter verbally, so there were no written patterns. Guernseys have had a slower revival in popularity than Arans, mainly because patterns have not been available and the 5-ply worsted wool, from which most genuine Guernseys should be made, is difficult to find. However in recent years the Channel Island Guernsey, usually machine-made, has become increasingly popular in Britain, and general interest in regional crafts has led to the formation of organisations such as the Northumbrian Craft Knitters' Association, which is devoted to the revival of the hand-knitted Guernsey.

Traditional Channel Island Guernsey

The best known Guernsey is that from the Channel Islands, recognisable by its side slits, diagonal gusset and insets of garter stitch and double rib. Traditionally, the main part is knitted in the round, but here the pattern has been adapted for two needles, with the ribbed neckband on four needles. However, a note is given on how to work the Guernsey in the round, if this is desired. The sleeves are worked separately, as is traditional with the Channel Island Guernsey.

The pattern is in 12 sizes, to fit 56cm (22 inch) to 112cm (44 inch) bust or chest. The Guernsey is knitted in traditional navy 5-ply worsted wool, which is manufactured especially for Guernsey sweaters. The yarn is also available in off-white, saxe blue and red.

ADULT SIZES

Materials: 15 (16:17:17:18:19) balls (50-gr) Poppleton Guernsey Wool 5-ply; two 2¾mm (No 12) needles; set of four 2¾mm (No 12) needles.

Measurements: To fit 86 (91:97:102:107:112)cm – 34 (36:38:40:42:44)in bust or chest; length, 63 (63:66:66:68:68)cm – 25 (25:26:26:27:27)ins; sleeve, 51 (51:53:53:56:56)cm – 20 (20:21:21:22:22)ins.

Tension: 14 sts and 18 rows to 5cm – 2ins over stocking stitch on 2¾mm (No 12) needles.

Abbreviations: See page 116.

Back and Front alike

With two 2¾mm (No 12) needles cast on 126 (134:140:148:154:162) sts. Work 20 rows g-st (every row k). Work 8 rows in k2, p2 rib, beg 2nd row p2 *for 1st, 2nd, 5th and 6th sizes only*.

Now work in st-st, beg k, until work measures 39 (39:41:41:42:42)cm – 15½ (15½:16:16:16½:16½:)ins from beg, ending p.

Next row: K.
Next row: P4, k8, p to last 12 sts, k8, p4.

Rep last 2 rows until work measures 63 (63:66:66:68:68)cm – 25 (25:26:26:27:27)ins from beg, ending with a wrong side row.

Shoulder Shaping: Cast off 37 (40:43:46:49:52) sts *loosely* at beg of next 2 rows. Leave 52 (54:54:56:56:58) sts on a spare needle.

Sleeves

With two 2¾mm (No 12) needles cast on 64 (64:68:68:72:72) sts. Work 8cm – 3ins in k2, p2 rib. Change to st-st and inc 1st each end every 5th row until there are 110 (110:118:118:126:126) sts. Cont straight until work measures 43 (43:46:46:48:48)cm – 17 (17:18:18:19:19)ins from beg, ending p.

Next row: Inc in first st, k to last 2 sts, inc in next st, k1. P1 row.
Next row: K1, inc in next st, k to last 3 sts, inc in next st, k2. P1 row.
Next row: K2, inc in next st, k to last 4 sts, inc in next st, k3. P1 row.
Next row: K3, inc in next st, k to last 5 sts, inc in next st, k4.

Inc in this way on every k row until 9 incs in all have been completed. P1 row.

Next row: K11, (p2, k2) to last 9 sts, k9.

Traditional Channel Island Guernsey

Next row: P11, (k2, p2) to last 9 sts, p9. Rep last 2 rows 3 times more*.

Next row: K10, cast off 108 (108:116:116:124: 124) sts *loosely* ribwise, k10.

Work on last 10 sts only in st-st, dec 1 st at inner edge on next 8 alternate rows. P2 tog. Fasten off. Complete 10 sts at other side to match.

Neckband

Join shoulders. With set of four $2\frac{3}{4}$mm (No 12) needles k sts from back neck then sts from front neck. 104 (108:108:112:112:116) sts. Work 10 rounds in k2, p2 rib. Cast off *loosely* ribwise.

Making up

Sew inner shaped edge of 10 side sts and ribbed band at top of sleeve to sides of back and front, beg and ending at start of g-st side bands. Join side and sleeve seams.

To make in the round

For all sizes a 40cm (16in) circular needle size $2\frac{3}{4}$mm (No 12) is required in addition to the two needles and set of four needles of the same size.

Back and Front alike

Work in two sections as given until 8 rows of rib are completed. Then place both sections on the circular needle and work in rounds of st-st (every round k) for the measurement given before the start of the side strips of 8 garter sts. Divide on to two needles and complete Back and Front as for the two-needle method.

Sleeves

With set of four needles cast on number of sts given and work in the round, placing increases in a straight line with one st between increases as a 'seam' marker. (Adult sizes only: change to the circular needle when 110 sts are reached.) After casting off top rib, revert to two needles.

The Neckband and Making Up will be the same as for the two-needle method, omitting the side and sleeve seam joins from the Making Up.

CHILDREN'S SIZES

Materials: 9 (10:11:12:13:14) balls (50-gr) Poppleton Guernsey Wool 5-ply; two $2\frac{3}{4}$mm (No 12) needles; a set of four $2\frac{3}{4}$mm (No 12) needles.

Measurements: To fit 56 (61:66:71:76:81)cm – 22 (24:26:28:30:32)in chest; length, 42 (46:49: 53:57:61)cm – $16\frac{1}{2}$ (18:$19\frac{1}{2}$:21:$22\frac{1}{2}$:24)ins; sleeve, 33 (37:41:43:46:48)cm – 13 ($14\frac{1}{2}$:16:17:18:19)ins.

Tension: 14 sts and 18 rows to 5cm – 2ins over stocking stitch on $2\frac{3}{4}$mm (No 12) needles.

Abbreviations: See page 116.

Back and Front alike

With two $2\frac{3}{4}$mm (No 12) needles cast on 84 (92:98:106:112:120)sts. Work 16 rows g-st (every row k). Work 8 rows in k2, p2 rib, beg 2nd row p2 *for 3rd and 4th sizes only*.
Now work in st-st, beg k, until work measures 25 (28:31:33:36:38)cm – 10 (11:12:13:14:15)ins from beg, ending p.
Next row: K.
Next row: P4, k8, p to last 12 sts, k8, p4.
Rep last 2 rows until work measures 42 (46:49: 53:57:61)cm – $16\frac{1}{2}$ (18:$19\frac{1}{2}$:21:$22\frac{1}{2}$:24)ins from beg, ending with a wrong side row.

Shoulder Shaping: Cast off 21 (24:26:29:31: 34)sts *loosely* at beg of next 2 rows. Leave 42 (44:46:48:50:52)sts on a spare needle.

Sleeves

With two $2\frac{3}{4}$mm (No 12) needles cast on 52 (56:56:60:60:60) sts. Work 8cm – 3ins in k2, p2 rib. Change to st-st and inc 1 st each end of every 5th row until there are 74 (82:86:94:98: 106) sts. Cont straight until work measures 25 (29:33:36:38:41)cm – 10 ($11\frac{1}{2}$:13:14:15:16)ins from beg, ending p.
Now work as Adult sizes from * to *.
Next row: K10, cast off 72 (80:84:92:96:104) sts *loosely* ribwise, k10.
Work on last 10 sts only in st-st, dec 1 st at inner edge on next 8 alternate rows. P2 tog. Fasten off. Complete 10 sts at other side to match.

Neckband

Join shoulders. With set of four $2\frac{3}{4}$mm (No 12) needles k sts from back neck then sts from front neck. 84 (88:92:96:100:104) sts. Work 10 rounds in k2, p2 rib. Cast off *loosely* ribwise.

Making Up

As Adult Sizes.

To make in the round

See Adult Sizes, above.

Scarborough Guernsey with Monogram

A classic Guernsey made in the traditional way on a circular needle, with four needles used for the neckband and lower part of the sleeves where the work is too narrow for one needle, and with the yoke worked on two needles. The sleeves have the typical Guernsey underarm gusset and are picked up from the yoke and worked downwards. The sweater is mainly in stocking stitch with a double moss stitch and ridge patterned yoke.

The pattern is in six sizes, to fit 81cm (32 inch) to 107cm (42 inch) bust or chest. The Guernsey is knitted in navy 5-ply worsted wool. (See also illustration page 85.)

Scarborough Guernsey with Monogram

Materials: 14 (14:15:16:17:18) balls (50-gr) Poppleton Guernsey Wool 5-ply; a 76cm (30in) and a 40cm (16in) circular needle size $2\frac{3}{4}$mm (No 12); set of four $2\frac{3}{4}$mm (No 12) needles; two $2\frac{3}{4}$mm (No 12) needles.

Measurements: To fit 81 (86:91:97:102:107)cm – 32 (34:36:38:40:42)ins bust or chest; length, 61 (61:63:63:66:66)cm – 24 (24:25:25:26:26)ins; sleeve, 43 (43:46:46:48:48)cm – 17 (17:18:18:19:19)ins.

Tension: 14 sts and 18 rows to 5cm – 2ins over stocking stitch on $2\frac{3}{4}$mm (No 12) needles.

Abbreviations: See page 116.

Monogram: The initials 'DM' are worked into this Guernsey above the front welt. To incorporate the letters of your choice, draw them on to squared paper, allowing approximately 10 sts and 16 rows for each letter, according to the letter's proportions. Then work the letters into the knitting above the front welt by working p for the letter sts and k for the background.

Main Part

With 76cm (30in) circular needle size $2\frac{3}{4}$mm (No 12) cast on 232 (248:264:280:296:312)sts.
Rounds 1 and 2: K.
Rounds 3 and 4: P. Rep last 4 rounds 5 times more.
Next round: *P2, k114 (122:130:138:146:154); rep from * once more.
Rep this round, thus working 2 p sts for each side edge, and incorporating initials after about 8 more rounds if required, until work measures 31 (31:32:32:33:33)cm – 12 (12:12½:12½:13:13)ins from beg.

Now work **Yoke** thus: P 2 rounds. Work 2 rounds k, keeping 2 p sts at each side. Rep last 4 rounds once more. Now shape thus:
1st round: *Inc in each of first 2 p sts, k2, p12, (k2, p2) 21 (23:25:27:29:31) times, k2, p12, k2; rep from * once more.
2nd round: *P1, k2, p1, k2, p12, (k2, p2) 21 (23: 25:27:29:31) times, k2, p12, k2; rep from * once more.
3rd round: *P1, k2, p1, k14, (p2, k2) 21 (23:25: 27:29:31) times, p2, k14; rep from * once more.

4th round: As 3rd.
These 4 rounds form patt for centre 114 (122: 130:138:146:154) sts for back and front, excluding 'p1, k2, p1' on each side edge.
Next round: *P1, inc in each of next 2 k sts, p1, patt 114 (122:130:138:146:154); rep from * once more.
Next round: *P1, k4, p1, patt 114 (122:130:138: 146:154); rep from * once more.
Cont in this way, inc 1 st each side of 'k' gusset between two side p sts on 3rd and every following 4th row until there are 20 sts in each k gusset. Work 1 round more, thus ending with a 2nd patt round.
***Next row:* With two $2\frac{3}{4}$mm (No 12) needles p1, k20, p1 and place these 22 sts on st holder, patt 114 (122:130:138:146:154) as 3rd round, TURN. Work on these sts only.
Next row: (wrong side). P14, (k2, p2) to last 16 sts, k2, p14.
Next row: K2, p12, (k2, p2) at last 16 sts, k2, p12, k2.
Next row: P2, k12, (p2, k2) to last 16 sts, p2, k12, p2.
Next row: K14, (p2, k2) to last 16 sts, p2, k14.
Rep these 4 rows until work measures 58 (58: 61:61:63:63)cm – 23 (23:24:24:25:25)ins from beg, ending with first of these 4 rows.

Neck Shaping: *Next row:* Patt 36 (40:43:47: 50:54), k2 tog, TURN. Work on these sts only, dec 1st at neck edge on next 3 rows. 34 (38: 41:45:48:52) sts.
Next row: P.
Next row: K.
Next row: K.
Next row: P.
Rep last 4 rows once more. Leave sts on spare needle. Place centre 38 (38:40:40:42:42) sts on st holder. Complete other side of neck.
Return to remaining sts and complete as first side from **.

Neckband

Graft shoulder sts of back and front yoke together. With set of four $2\frac{3}{4}$mm (No 12) needles (k sts from one st holder, pick up and k 16 sts around side of neck) twice. 108 (108:112:112: 116:116) sts. Work 11 rounds in k2, p2 rib. Cast off loosely ribwise.

Sleeves

With 40cm (16in) circular needle size $2\frac{3}{4}$mm (No 12) work p1, k20, p1 across one set of gusset sts then pick up and k100 (100:106:106: 112:112) sts evenly around yoke edge.

Next round: P1, k20, p1, k to end.

Next round: P1, k2 tog, k16, k2 tog, p1, k to end.

Cont in this way, dec 1 st each end of k gusset on every 4th round until 2 sts remain in gusset. Work 3 rounds.

Next round: (P2 tog) twice, k to end.

Cont with 2 underarm sts in p and dec 1 st each side of 2 p sts on every 5th round until 72 (72: 76:76:80:80) sts remain, changing to set of four $2\frac{3}{4}$mm (No 12) needles after 112 sts.

Now work in rounds of k2, p2 rib until sleeve measures 43 (43:46:46:48:48)cm – 17 (17: 18:18:19:19)ins from beg. Cast off ribwise.

Monogram detail on Scarborough Guernsey

Flamborough Guernsey

An intricately patterned Guernsey, with panels of net mask, diamond, cable and moss stitch on the back and front. The sleeves are mainly in stocking stitch with a square of pattern at the centre top. The sleeves have a ribbed saddle shoulder extension that is sewn between the shoulders and joined to the ribbed neckband. All borders are in double rib.

The pattern is in six sizes, to fit 86cm (34 inch) to 112cm (44 inch) bust or chest. The Guernsey is knitted in navy 5-ply worsted wool.

Flamborough Guernsey

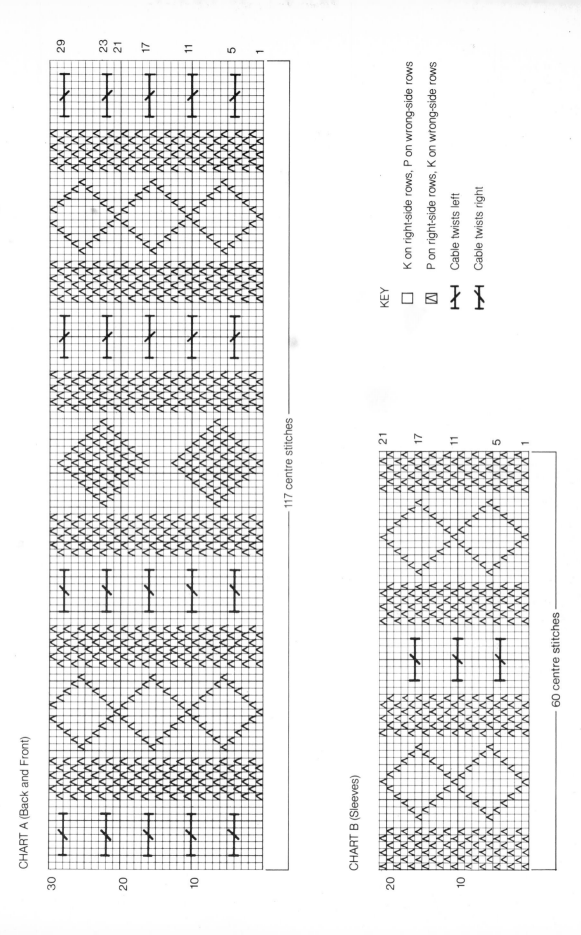

CHART A (Back and Front)

29
23
21
17
11
5
1

30

20

10

117 centre stitches

CHART B (Sleeves)

21

17

11

5

1

20

10

60 centre stitches

KEY

☐   K on right-side rows, P on wrong-side rows

▨   P on right-side rows, K on wrong-side rows

⎠   Cable twists left

⎡   Cable twists right

Materials: 13 (14:15:16:16:17) balls (50-gr) Poppleton Guernsey Wool 5-ply; two 2¾mm (No 12) needles; set of four 2¾mm (No 12) needles; cable needle.

Measurements: To fit 86 (91:97:102:107: 122)cm – 34 (36:38:40:42:44)in bust or chest; length, 61 (63:63:66:66:68)cm – 24 (25:25:26:26: 27)ins; sleeve, 51 (51:53:53:56:56)cm – 20 (20: 21:21:22:22)ins.

Tension: 14 sts and 18 rows to 5cm – 2ins over stocking stitch on 2¾mm (No 12) needles.

Abbreviations: See page 116.

Back and Front alike

With two 2¾mm (No 12) needles cast on 122 (130:138:146:150:158) sts. Work 14cm – 5½ins in k2, p2 rib, beg 2nd row p2 and inc 1 st at end of last row. 123 (131:139:147:151:159) sts. Work 4cm – 1½ins in st-st, beg k and ending p.

Now work chart A patt thus:

For centre 117 sts: Work patt from chart, working two right-hand 6-st cables thus: place next 3 sts on cable needle and leave at *front* of work, k3 then k3 from cable needle. For two left-hand 6-st cables work thus: place next 3 sts on cable needle and leave at *back* of work, k3 then k3 from cable needle.

For remaining 6 (14:22:30:34:42) sts: Work as 3 (7:11:15:17:21)-st m-st borders, beg and ending each border and each row with k1. Work patt in this way until work measures 58 (61:61:63:63:66)cm – 23 (24:24:25:25:26)ins from beg, ending with a wrong side row.

Shoulder Shaping: Cast off 38 (41:44:47:49: 52) sts *loosely* at beg of next 2 rows. Leave centre 47 (49:51:53:53:55) sts on spare needle.

Sleeves

With two 2¾mm (No 12) needles cast on 52 (56: 56:60:60:64) sts. Work 9cm – 3½ins in k2, p2 rib. Cont in st-st, inc 1 st each end of 2nd and every following 4th row until work measures 36 (36:38:38:41:41)cm – 14 (14:15:15:16:16)ins from beg, ending p. Still inc at side edges as before until there are 122 (130:130:136:136: 142) sts and working side sts in st-st, place 60 sts of chart B at centre of work and cont until 6 diamonds are completed. Work should now measure 51 (51:53:53:56:56)cm – 20 (20: 21:21:22:22)ins.

Now cast off 53 (57:57:60:60:63) sts *loosely* at beg of next 2 rows. 16 sts. Work 14 (14½:16: 17:17:19)cm – 5½ (5¾:6¼:6¾:7:7½)ins in k2, p2 rib for saddle shoulder. Leave sts on spare needle.

Neckband

Sew saddle shoulder extensions between shoulder shapings of back and front. With set of four 2¾mm (No 12) needles rib 16 sts of left sleeve, k sts from front, inc 1 (3:1:3:3:1) sts across row, rib 16 sts from right sleeve, k sts from back inc as for front. 128 (136:136:144: 144:144) sts. Work 8 rounds in k2, p2 rib. Cast off *loosely* ribwise.

Making up

Join cast-off edges of sleeves to sides of back and front. Join side and sleeve seams.

Scots Fishing Fleet Guernsey

A fine Scottish Guernsey with panels of anchor, marriage lines, wave and diamond patterns. The pattern repeats are of different lengths and so each panel must be followed individually. The sleeves are in stocking stitch with cuffs and top bands in double rib. The welt and neckband are also in double rib.

The pattern is in three sizes, to fit 86cm (34 inch), 94cm (37 inch) and 102cm (40 inch) bust or chest. The 8cm (3 inch) gap between sizes is due to the wide pattern repeat. The Guernsey is knitted in standard double knitting wool. (See illustration also page 33.)

Scots Fishing Fleet Guernsey

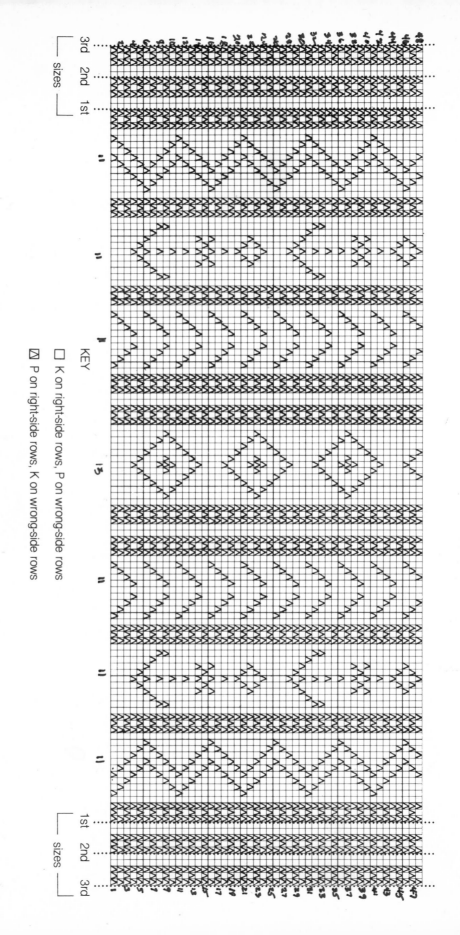

KEY

☐ K on right-side rows, P on wrong-side rows

☒ P on right-side rows, K on wrong-side rows

Materials: 24 (26:28) balls (25-gr) Double Knitting Wool in Black; two each 3¼mm (No 10) and 2¾mm (No 12) needles.

Measurements: To fit 86 (94:102)cm – 34 (37: 40)in bust or chest; length, 63 (66:68)cm – 25 (26:27)ins; sleeve, 46 (48:51)cm – 18 (19:20)ins.

Tension: 13 sts and 17 rows to 5cm – 2ins over stocking stitch on 3¼mm (No 10) needles.

Abbreviations: See page 116.

Back and Front alike

With 2¾mm (No 12) needles cast on 112 (122: 132) sts. Work 8cm – 3ins in k2, p2 rib, beg 2nd row p2 *for 2nd size only*, and inc. 1 st at end of last row. 113 (123:133) sts. Change to 3¼mm (No 10) needles. Work 10 rows st-st, beg k.

Now work patt from chart, keeping continuity of each panel and working 5 sts extra at side edge for each of two larger sizes as shown, until work measures 63 (66:68)cm – 25 (26:27)ins from beg, ending with a wrong side row.

Shoulder Shaping: Cast off 33 (38:43) sts *loosely* at beg of next 2 rows. 47 sts.

Next row: K2, (inc in next st, k2) to end. 62 sts.

Change to 2¾mm (No 12) needles and work 7 rows in *p2, k2* rib, beg 2nd row k2. Cast off *loosely* ribwise.

Sleeves

With 2¾mm (No 12) needles cast on 64(68:68) sts. Work 8cm – 3ins in k2, p2 rib. Change to 3¼mm (No 10) needles. Cont in st-st, inc 1 st each end of every 4th row until there are 122 (126:130) sts.

Cont straight until work measures 41 (43: 46)cm – 16 (17:18)ins from beg, ending p. Now work 5cm – 2ins in k2, p2 rib, beg 2nd row p2. Cast off *loosely* ribwise.

R 120

Making up

Press lightly, omitting rib. Join shoulder and neckband seams. Sew cast-off edges of sleeves to sides of back and front, beg and ending 20 (22:23)cm – 8 (8½:9)ins from shoulder seams. Join side and sleeve seams. Press seams.

Whitby Guernsey

A very simple Guernsey, made up of four straight pieces with no shaping. The back and front are alike with a slit neck and a double moss stitch and ridge patterned yoke. The sleeves are also straight, with a top pattern to match the yoke. The main body of the garment is in stocking stitch with ridge patterned borders.

The pattern is in six sizes, to fit 86cm (34 inch) to 112cm (44 inch) bust or chest. The Guernsey is knitted in Aran wool.

Whitby Guernsey

Opposite: *Shetland Cardigan (page 107) and Scots Fishing Fleet Guernsey (page 29)*

Materials: 14 (15:16:17:17:18) balls (50-gr) Aran Wool; two 4mm (No 8) needles.

Measurements: To fit 86 (91:97:102:107: 122)cm — 34 (36:38:40:42:44)in bust or chest; length, 61 (61:63:63:66:68)cm — 24 (24:25:25: 26:27)ins; sleeve, 38 (38:41:43:46:48)cm — 15 (15:16:17:18:19)ins.

Tension: 10 sts and 13 rows to 5cm — 2ins over stocking stitch on 4mm (No 8) needles.

Abbreviations: See page 116.

Back and Front alike

With 4mm (No 8) needles cast on 90 (94:98: 106:110:114) sts.
1st row: (right side). K.
2nd row: P.
3rd row: P.
4th row: K.
These 4 rows form ridge patt. Work 8 rows more in ridge patt.

Now cont in st-st, beg k, until work measures 31 (31:33:33:36:38)cm — 12 (12:13:13:14:15)ins from beg, ending p.

Now work **Yoke** thus: Work 10 rows in ridge patt, beg with a 3rd row.
11th row: K10, p2, (k2, p2) to last 10 sts, k10.
12th row: P10, k2 (p2, k2) to last 10 sts, p10.
13th row: As 12th.
14th row: As 11th.

Rep last 4 rows 4 times more then 11th and 12th rows again. These 32 rows form yoke patt.

Rep first 28 rows of yoke patt again then rep first 24 rows of yoke patt – thus making patt rep shorter by 4 rows each time. Now rep first 10 rows again. Cast off *loosely* knitwise.

Sleeves

With 4mm (No 8) needles cast on 80 (80:84:84: 88:92) sts. Work 12 rows in ridge patt as Back and Front. Now work in st-st, beg k, until work measures 28 (28:31:33:36:38)cm — 11 (11: 12:13:14:15)ins from beg, ending p.

Now work sleeve top patt thus: Work 12 rows in ridge patt, beg with a 3rd row.
13th row: (K2, p2) to end.
14th row: As 13th.
15th row: (P2, k2) to end.
16th row: As 15th.

Rep last 4 rows once more then 13th and 14th rows again. Work 14 rows in ridge patt, beg with a 1st row. Cast off *loosely* knitwise.

Making up

Press lightly. Join shoulders, leaving approx 28cm — 11ins open for head. Sew cast-off edges of sleeves to sides of back and front, beg and ending 20 (20:22:22:24:25)cm — 8 (8:8½:8½:9½: 10)ins from shoulder seams. Join side and sleeve seams. Press seams lightly.

Opposite: Aran Crew Neck Sweater (page 63) and Faroe Island Sweater (page 110)

Inverness Guernsey

A thick Guernsey with an all-over pattern on the back and front, including flag and bar patterns on the body with chevron, diamond and double moss stitch panels on the yoke. The sleeves are mainly stocking stitch with a centre panel of rib and moss stitch. The neckband and cuffs are ribbed.

The pattern is in four sizes, to fit 86cm (34 inch) to 102cm (40 inch) bust or chest. The Guernsey is knitted in Aran wool.

Inverness Guernsey

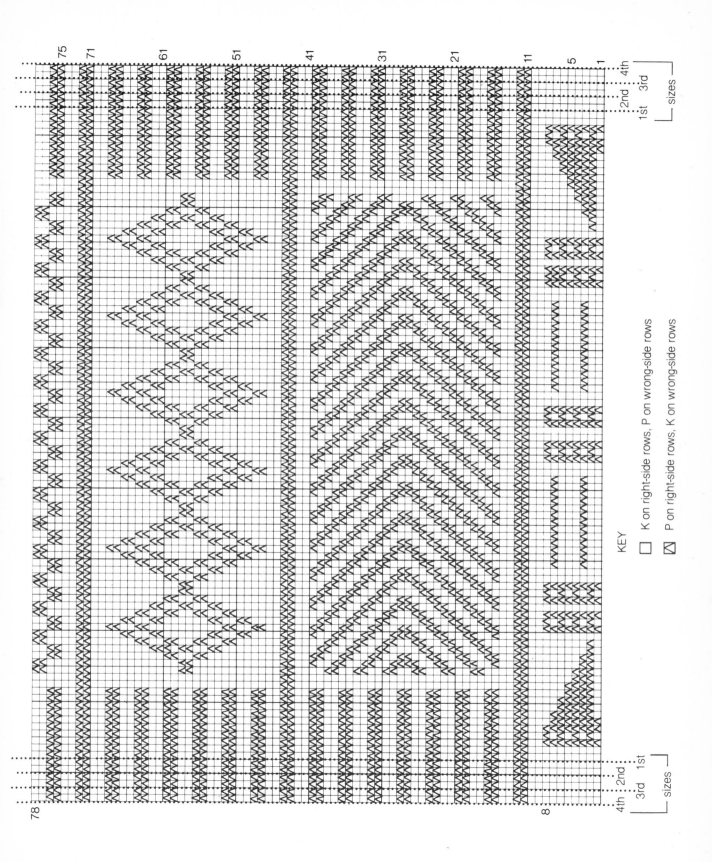

KEY

☐ K on right-side rows, P on wrong-side rows

☒ P on right-side rows, K on wrong-side rows

Materials: 15 (17:18:20) balls (50-gr) Aran Wool; two 4mm (No 8) needles.

Measurements: To fit 86 (91:97:102)cm − 34 (36:38:40)in bust or chest; length, 61 (64:67: 67)cm − 24 (25¼:26½:26½)ins; sleeve, 43 (46:48: 48)cm − 17 (18:19:19)ins.

Tension: 10 sts and 13 rows to 5cm − 2ins over stocking stitch on 4mm (No 8) needles.

Abbreviations: See page 116.

Back and Front alike

With 4mm (No 8) needles cast on 92 (96:100: 104) sts.
1st row: (right side). K.
2nd row: P.
3rd row: P.
4th row: K.
These 4 rows form ridge patt. Work 6 rows more in ridge patt.

Now work patt from chart, rep 1st to 8th rows 10 (11:12:12) times, keeping 2 (4:6:8) sts at each side edge in st-st as shown on the chart.

Now work 9th to 78th rows of chart, then rep 75th to 78th rows 3 times more, then rep 75th and 76th rows.

Work 6 rows in ridge patt, beg with a 1st row.

Shoulder Shaping row: Cast off 26 (28:30:32) sts *loosely* knitwise, k40, cast off remaining 26 (28:30:32) sts *loosely* knitwise.

Neckband

Rejoin yarn to centre 40 sts and work 8 rows in k1, p1 rib. Cast off *loosely* ribwise.

Sleeves

With 4mm (No 8) needles cast on 44 (48:52:52) sts. Work 8cm − 3ins in k2, p2 rib. Now work thus:
1st row: (right side). K18 (20:22:22), p1, k1, p1, k2, p1, k1, p1, k18 (20:22:22).
2nd row: P18 (20:22:22), k3, p2, k3, p18 (20: 22:22).
These 2 rows form st-st with 10-st centre panel. Keeping centre panel in line, inc 1 st each end of next and every following 4th row until there are 84 (90:96:96) sts, working extra sts into st-st.

Cont straight until work measures 41 (43: 46:46)cm − 16(17:18:18)ins from beg, ending p. Now work 8 rows in ridge patt, beg with a 3rd row. Cast off *loosely* knitwise.

Making up

Press lightly. Join shoulder and neckband seams. Sew cast-off edges of sleeves to sides of back and front, beg and ending 22 (23:24:24)cm − 8½ (9:9½:9½)ins from shoulder seams. Join side and sleeve seams. Press seams.

Hebridean Guernsey

An intricately patterned Guernsey, with panels of flag and zig-zag marriage lines on the body of the back and front, and a combination of tree of life and diamond motifs with cable and herringbone panels on the yoke. The sleeves are in stocking stitch and all the borders are ribbed.

The pattern is in four sizes, to fit 86cm (34 inch) to 102cm (40 inch) bust or chest. The Guernsey is knitted in off-white 5-ply worsted wool – the traditional colour for a Hebridean garment.

Hebridean Guernsey

Materials: 12 (13:14:15) balls (50-gr) Poppleton Guernsey Wool 5-ply; two $2\frac{3}{4}$mm (No 12) needles; cable needle.

Measurements: To fit 86 (91:97:102)cm – 34 (36:38:40)in bust or chest; length, 61 (61:68:68)cm – 24 (24:27:27)ins; sleeve, 51 (53:56:56)cm – 20 (21:22:22)ins.

Tension: 14 sts and 18 rows to 5cm – 2ins over stocking stitch on $2\frac{3}{4}$mm (No 12) needles.

Abbreviations: See page 116.

Back and Front alike

With $2\frac{3}{4}$mm (No 12) needles cast on 135 (141:149:155) sts. Work 10cm – 4ins in k1, p1 rib, beg 2nd row pl. Now work from chart A thus:

For centre 133 sts: Rep 26-st rep of chart 5 times in each row, working 3 sts beyond dotted line at end of k rows and beg of p rows only.

For 1 (4:8:11) sts at each end of every row: Work in st-st throughout.

Cont from chart A until 4 (4:5:5) chart reps are completed.

Yoke: Now work ridge patt thus:
1st row: (right side). K.
2nd row: P.
3rd row: P.
4th row: K.
  Now work 79 rows of chart B, placing 133 sts of chart at centre with 1 (4:8:11) sts at each side edge in st-st as before, and working cables on 5th and every following 6th row thus:
For two right-hand cables: place first 3 sts on cable needle and leave at *front* of work, k3 then k3 from cable needle.
For two left-hand cables: place first 3 sts on cable needle and leave at *back* of work, k3 then k3 from cable needle.
  When 79 rows of chart B are completed p 1 row then work 4 rows in ridge patt, beg with a 1st row.

Neck Dividing row: K42 (45:49:52), TURN. Work on these sts only. Work 5 rows more in ridge patt. Cast off *loosely* knitwise. Place centre 51 sts on a st holder, rejoin yarn and k42 (45:49:52) to end. Complete to match other side.

Sleeves

With $2\frac{3}{4}$mm (No 12) needles cast on 58 (58:64:64) sts. Work 10cm – 4ins in k1, p1 rib. Cont in st-st, inc 1 st each end of every 4th row until there are 120 (120:132:132) sts. Cont straight until work measures 51 (53:56:56)cm – 20 (21:22:22)ins from beg. Cast off *loosely*.

Neckband

Join right shoulder. With $2\frac{3}{4}$mm (No. 12) needles pick up and k 5 sts down left side of front neck, k sts from st holder, pick up and k 5 sts up right side of front neck and 5 sts down right side of back neck, k sts from st holder, pick up and k 5 sts up left side of back neck. 122 sts. Work 10 rows in k1, p1 rib. Cast off *loosely* ribwise.

Making up

Join left shoulder and neckband seam. Sew cast-off edges of sleeves to sides of back and front, beg and ending 22 (22:24:24)cm – $8\frac{1}{2}$ ($8\frac{1}{2}$:$9\frac{1}{2}$:$9\frac{1}{2}$)ins from shoulder seams. Join side and sleeve seams.

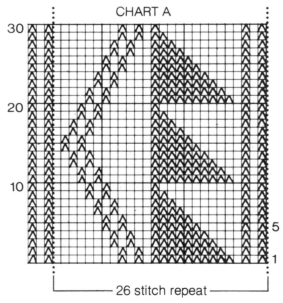

CHART A

30

20

10

5

1

— 26 stitch repeat —

KEY

☐ K on right-side rows, P on wrong-side rows

◩ P on right-side rows, K on wrong-side rows

CHART B

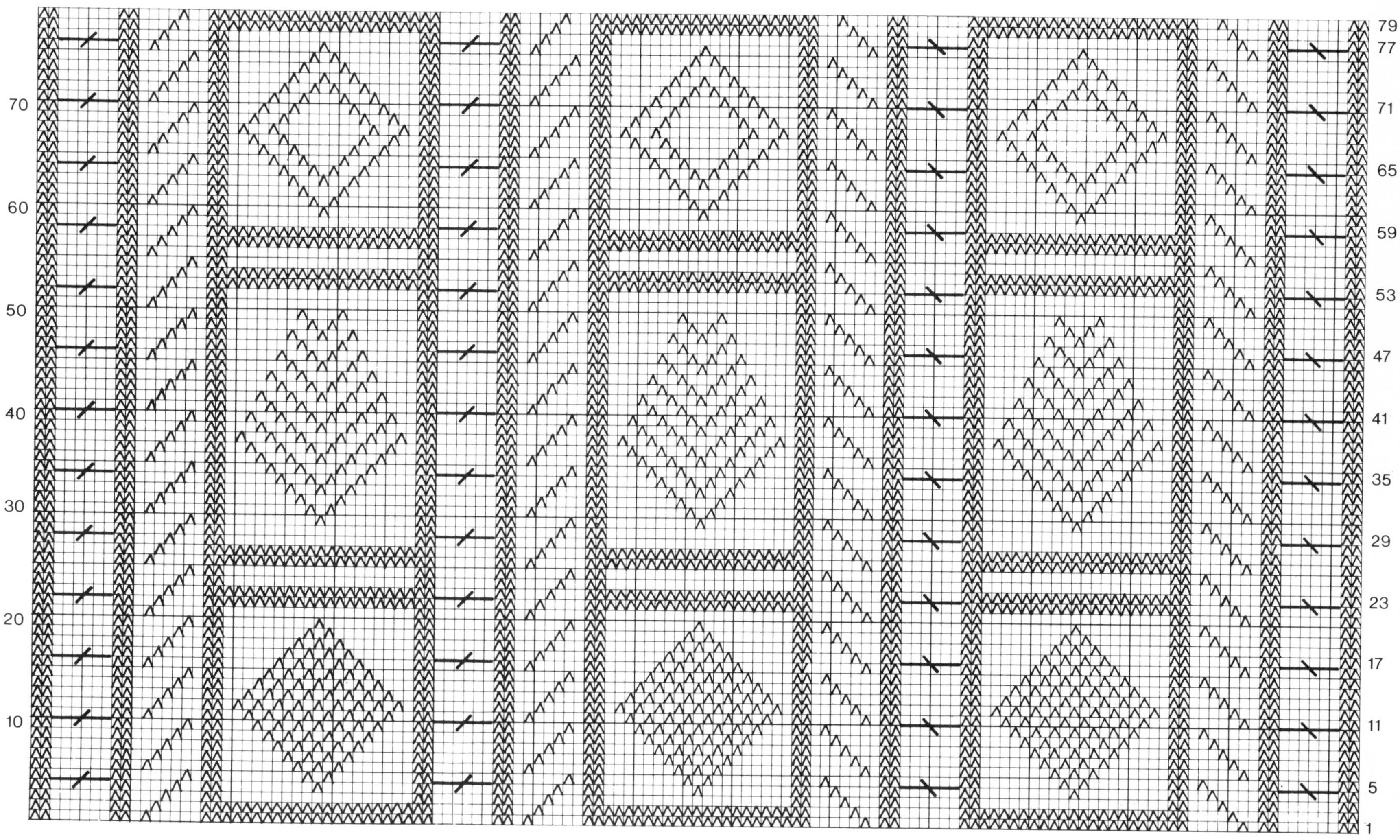

KEY

☐ K on right-side rows, P on wrong-side rows

☒ P on right-side rows, K on wrong-side rows

╪ Cable twists left

╳ Cable twists right

Child's Lerwick Guernsey

A thick Guernsey with a patterned yoke showing vertical lines of lightning zig-zag, moss stitch and double rib. The main body and sleeves are worked in stocking stitch, the neckband and cuffs are ribbed and the lower border is in garter stitch.

The pattern is in five sizes, to fit 56cm (22 inch) to 86cm (34 inch) chest. The Guernsey is knitted in Aran wool.

Child's Lerwick Guernsey

Materials: 8 (10:11:13:14) balls (50-gr) Aran Wool; two 4mm (No 8) needles.

Measurements: To fit 56 (63:71:79:86)cm – 22 (25:28:31:34)in chest; length, 38 (43:48:53:58)cm – 15 (17:19:21:23)ins; sleeve, 31 (34: 38: 42:46)cm – 12 (13½:15:16½:18)ins.

Tension: 10 sts and 13 rows to 5cm – 2ins over stocking stitch on 4mm (No 8) needles.

Abbreviations: See page 116.

Back

With 4mm (No 8) needles cast on 59 (67:75:83:91) sts. Work 10 rows g-st (every row k). Cont in st-st, beg k, until work measures 23 (23:28:28:33)cm – 9 (9:11:11:13)ins from beg, ending p.

Now work yoke patt thus: Work 6 rows g-st. Now work 55 sts of chart at centre of work with 2 (6:10:14:18) sts each side of chart in p2, k2 rib, beg wrong side rows k2 (note: for first size work p2 each end of right-side rows and k2 each end of wrong side rows). Work 14 rows of chart 2 (3:3:4:4) times then first 4 rows again*. Work 8 rows g-st.

Shoulder Shaping row: Cast off 15 (18:20:22:25) sts *loosely* knitwise, k29 (31:35:39:41), cast off remaining 15 (18:20:22:25) sts *loosely* knitwise.

Front

As Back to *. Work 2 rows g-st.

Neck Shaping: *Next row:* K17 (20:22:24:27), k2 tog, TURN. Work on these sts only in g-st, dec 1 st at neck edge on next 3 rows. Work 2 rows straight in g-st. Cast off *loosely* knitwise. Place centre 21 (23:27:31:33) sts on a st holder. Complete other side of neck to match.

Sleeves

With 4mm (No 8) needles cast on 34 (36:38:40:42) sts. Work 6cm – 2½ins in k1 tbl, p1 rib.

Now work in st-st, inc 1 st each end of every 4th row until there are 60 (66:70:76:80) sts. Cont in st-st until work measures 31 (34:38:42:46)cm – 12 (13½:15:16½:18)ins from beg. Cast off *loosely*.

Neckband

Join right shoulder. With 4mm (No 8) needles pick up and k 6 sts down left side of front neck, k sts from st holder, pick up and k 6 sts up right side of front neck then k sts from back neck. 62 (66:74:82:86) sts. Work 7 rows in k1, p1 rib. Cast off *loosely* ribwise.

Making up

Press lightly. Join left shoulder and neckband seam. Sew cast-off edges of sleeves to sides of back and front, beg and ending 15 (17:18:19:20)cm – 6 (6½:7:7½:8)ins from shoulder seams. Join side and sleeve seams. Press seams.

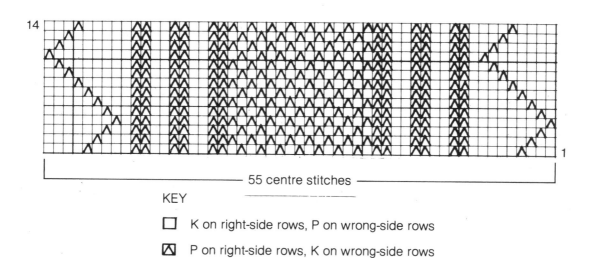

14   1

— 55 centre stitches —

KEY

☐ K on right-side rows, P on wrong-side rows

◪ P on right-side rows, K on wrong-side rows

Child's Filey Guernsey

A child's Guernsey made in the traditional way on a circular needle and set of four needles, with the yoke worked on two needles. The sleeves are picked up from the side edges of the yoke and worked downwards on four needles as the child-size sleeves are too narrow for a circular needle. The yoke is worked in a simple pattern of zig-zags, bars and double moss stitch and the remainder of the garment is in stocking stitch with double rib borders.

The pattern is in four sizes, to fit 56cm (22 inch) to 71cm (28 inch) chest. The Guernsey is knitted in navy 5-ply worsted wool. (See also illustration page 53.)

Child's Filey Guernsey

Materials: 9 (10:11:12) balls (50-gr) Poppleton Guernsey Wool 5-ply; a 40cm (16in) circular needle size 2¾mm (No 12); set of four 2¾mm (No 12) needles; two 2¾mm (No 12) needles.

Measurements: To fit 56 (61:66:71)cm – 22 (24:26:28)in chest; length, 39 (43:47:51)cm – 15½ (17:18½:20)ins; sleeve, 28 (32:36:39)cm – 11 (12½:14:15½)ins.

Tension: 14 sts and 18 rows to 5cm – 2ins over stocking stitch on 2¾mm (No 12) needles.

Abbreviations: See page 116.

Main Part

With 2¾mm (No 12) circular needle cast on 168 (184:200:216) sts. Work 5cm – 2ins in rounds of k2, p2 rib.

Next round: *P1, k83 (91:99:107); rep from * once. Rep this round, thus working in st-st with a p st for each side edge, until work measures 23 (25:28:31)cm – 9(10:11:12)ins from beg.

Next round: Cast off 1, k83 (91:99:107), cast off 1, k to end.

Work on last set of sts for **Front Yoke**. Change to two 2¾mm (No 12) needles.

Now work from chart thus:

1st row: (right side). (K2, p2) 4 (5:6:7) times, work 51 sts of 1st row of chart, (p2, k2) 4 (5:6:7) times.

2nd row: (P2, k2) 4 (5:6:7) times, work 51 sts of 2nd row of chart, (k2, p2) 4 (5:6:7) times.

3rd row: (P2, k2) 4 (5:6:7) times, work 51 sts of 3rd row of chart, (k2, p2) 4 (5:6:7) times.

4th row: (K2, p2) 4 (5:6:7) times, work 51 sts of 4th row of chart, (p2, k2) 4 (5:6:7) times.

Rep these 4 rows for double m-st on 16(20:24:28) sts at each side and work chart patt until work measures 39 (43:47:51)cm – 15½ (17:18½:20)ins from beg, ending with a wrong side row.

Shoulder Shaping: Cast off 24 (26:29:31) sts *loosely* at beg of next 2 rows. Leave 35 (39:41:45) sts on a spare needle.

Rejoin yarn to remaining 83 (91:99:107) sts for **Back Yoke** and work exactly as front yoke.

Neckband

Join shoulders. With set of four 2¾mm (No 12) needles k sts from front neck, inc 1 st at centre, then k sts from back neck, inc 1 st at centre. 72 (80:84:92)sts. Work 8 rounds in k2, p2 rib. Cast off *loosely* ribwise.

Sleeves

With set of four 2¾mm (No 12) needles beg at top of side edge and pick up and k 1 st from cast-off 1 p st, 45 (49:52:56) sts up side of yoke to shoulder then 45 (49:52:56) sts down other side of yoke. 91 (99:105:113) sts.

1st round: P1, k to end.

Keeping 1 st p, cont in st-st, dec 1 st each end of p st on every 3rd round until 37 (41:45:49) sts remain. Work 3 rounds more, dec 1 st at centre of last round. 36 (40:44:48) sts.

Now work in rounds of k2, p2 rib until sleeve measures 28 (31:36:39)cm – 11 (12½:14: 15½)ins from beg. Cast off ribwise.

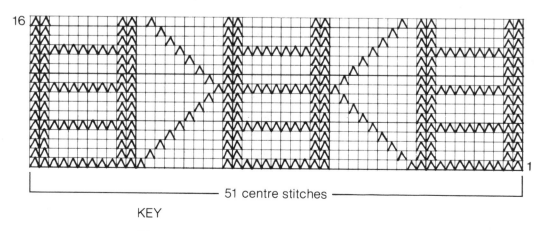

16

1

├── 51 centre stitches ──┤

KEY

☐ K on right-side rows, P on wrong-side rows

◩ P on right-side rows, K on wrong-side rows

Child's Guernsey Duffle Jacket

A warm, duffle-style jacket for a very small child. The main part is worked in a large diamond pattern, the sleeves and yoke are in moss stitch and a ridge pattern is used for the borders. The toggle strings are also knitted.

   The pattern is in one size only, to fit 51–56cm (20–22 inch) chest. The jacket is knitted in Aran wool.

Child's Guernsey Duffle Jacket

Materials: 5 balls (50-gr) Aran Wool; two 4mm (No 8) needles; 4 small wooden toggles.

Measurements: To fit 51–56cm – 20–22in chest; length, 33cm – 13ins; sleeve, 15cm – 6ins.

Tension: 10 sts and 14 rows to 5cm – 2ins over stocking stitch on 4mm (No 8) needles.

Abbreviations: See page 116.

Main Part

With 4mm (No 8) needles cast on 129 sts.

1st row: (right side). K.

2nd row: P.

3rd row: P.

4th row: K.

These 4 rows form ridge patt. Work 10 rows more in ridge patt.

Now work diamond patt thus:

1st row: (right side). P4, k9, (p3, k17) 5 times, p3, k9, p4.

2nd row: K4, p9, (k3, p17) 5 times, k3, p9, k4.

3rd row: K12, (p2, k1, p2, k15) 5 times, p2, k1, p2, k12.

4th row: P11, (k2, p3, k2, p13) 5 times, k2, p3, k2, p11.

5th row: P4, k6, (p2, k5, p2, k11) 5 times, p2, k5, p2, k6, p4.

6th row: K4, p5, (k2, p7, k2, p9) 5 times, k2, p7, k2, p5, k4.

7th row: K8, (p2, k9, p2, k7) 5 times, p2, k9, p2, k8.

8th row: P7, (k2, p11, k2, p5) 5 times, k2, p11, k2, p7.

9th row: P4, k2, (p2, k13, p2, k3) 5 times, p2, k13, p2, k2, p4.

10th row: K4, p1, (k2, p15, k2, p1) 5 times, k2, p15, k2, p1, k4.

11th row: K4, p2, (k17, p3) 5 times, k17, p2, k4.

12th row: P4, k2 (p17, k3) 5 times, p17, k2, p4.

13th row: P4, k1, (p2, k15, p2, k1) 6 times, p4.

14th row: K4, p2, (k2, p13, k2, p3) 5 times, k2, p13, k2, p2, k4.

15th row: K7, (p2, k11, p2, k5) 5 times, p2, k11, p2, k7.

16th row: P8, (k2, p9, k2, p7) 5 times, k2, p9, k2, p8.

17th row: P4, k5, (p2, k7, p2, k9) 5 times, p2, k7, p2, k5, p4.

18th row: K4, p6, (k2, p5, k2, p11) 5 times, k2, p5, k2, p6, k4.

19th row: K11, (p2, k3, p2, k13) 5 times, p2, k3, p2, k11.

20th row: P12, (k2, p1, k2, p15) 5 times, k2, p1, k2, p12.

These 20 rows form diamond patt with front borders. Rep last 20 rows once more then 1st and 2nd rows again.

Now work 10 rows in ridge patt, beg with a 1st row.

M-st row: P4, k1, (p1, k1) to last 4 sts, p4.

Next row: K5, (p1, k1) to last 4 sts, k4.

These 2 rows form m-st with 4-st front borders.

Armhole Dividing row: K4, m-st 28, cast off 6 sts for right armhole, m-st 53, cast off 6 sts for left armhole, m-st 28, k4. Work on last set of sts for **Left Front.** Cont in m-st with 4 sts at front edge in ridge patt as before and dec 1 st at armhole edge at beg of every alternate row until 20 sts remain, ending at armhole edge.

Neck Shaping: *Next row:* (right side). K2 tog, m-st 8, k2 tog, turn and place remaining 8 sts on a safety pin. Cont in m-st dec 1 st each end of next 4 alternate rows. P2 tog. Fasten off.

Rejoin yarn to centre 53 sts for **Back.** Cont in m-st, dec 1 st each end of every alternate row until 19 sts remain, ending with a wrong side row. Leave sts on spare needle.

Rejoin yarn to wrong side of remaining 32 sts for **Right Front.** Cont in m-st with 4 sts at front edge in ridge patt, dec 1 st at armhole edge at end of every alternate row until 20 sts remain, ending at front edge.

Neck Shaping: *Next row:* K8 and place these 8 sts on a safety pin, k2 tog, m-st 8, k2 tog. Cont in m-st, dec 1 st each end of next 4 alternate rows. P2 tog. Fasten off.

Sleeves

With 4mm (No 8) needles cast on 43 sts. Work 14 rows in ridge patt as Main Part.

M-st row: K1, (p1, k1) to end.

Cont in m-st until work measures 15cm – 6ins from beg.

Top Shaping: Cast off 3 sts at beg of next 2 rows. Cont in m-st, dec 1 st each end of next and every following alternate row until 3 sts remain. Leave sts on spare needle.

Neckband

Join raglan armhole seams. Place 8 sts at right front edge on to a 4mm (No 8) needle, then pick up and k 7 sts around right side of front neck, k sts from right sleeve, back and left sleeve, pick up and k 7 sts around left side of front neck, then k 8 sts from safety pin. 55 sts. Work 5 rows in ridge patt, beg with a 2nd row. Cast off knitwise.

Toggle Bands

(2 alike). With 4mm (No 8) needles cast on 30 sts then cast off.

Making up

Join sleeve seams. Sew 4 toggles to each front as shown, then sew doubled toggle bands to right front for a girl and to left front for a boy.

Baby's Guernsey

A Guernsey designed especially for a baby in a soft but hard-wearing wool. The yoke and top-sleeve pattern is a simple combination of double moss stitch and bar-ridge rows. The main parts of back, front and sleeves are in stocking stitch with ribbed borders.

The pattern is in two sizes, to fit 46cm (18 inch) and 51cm (20 inch) chest. The Guernsey is knitted in Shetland 2-ply Lace Weight wool, which is a 4-ply equivalent.

Baby's Guernsey

Materials: 2 (3) hanks (1-oz) Shetland 2-ply Lace Weight Wool; two each $2\frac{3}{4}$mm (No 12) and $2\frac{1}{4}$mm (No 13) needles; 4 buttons.

Measurements: To fit 46 (51)cm – 18 (20)in chest; length, 25 (28)cm – 10 (11)ins; sleeve, 15 (18)cm – 6 (7)ins.

Tension: 16 sts and 24 rows to 5cm – 2ins over stocking stitch on $2\frac{3}{4}$mm (No 12) needles.

Abbreviations: See page 116.

Back

With $2\frac{1}{4}$mm (No 13) needles cast on 78 (86) sts. Work 10 rows in k1, p1 rib. Change to $2\frac{3}{4}$mm (No 12) needles.
11th row: (right side). K.
12th row: P.
13th row: P.
14th row: K.
Rep last 4 rows twice more.
Now cont in st-st, beg k, until work measures 14 (17)cm – $5\frac{1}{2}$ ($6\frac{1}{2}$)ins from beg, ending p.
  Now work **Yoke** patt thus:
1st row: (right side). P.
2nd row: K.
3rd row: K.
4th row: P.
Rep last 4 rows once.
9th row: P8, k2, (p2, k2) to last 8 sts, p8.
10th row: K8, p2, (k2, p2) to last 8 sts, k8.
11th row: As 10th.
12th row: As 9th.
Rep last 4 rows 3 times more.
25th row: K.
26th row: P.
Rep last 26 rows once more *.

Now rep 1st to 4th rows inclusive of yoke patt 3 times more. Cast off *loosely* knitwise.

Front

As Back to *. P 1 row, k 1 row.

Neck Shaping row: K26 (29), cast off centre 26 (28) sts knitwise, k26 (29). Work on last set of sts only. P 1 row.

Now rep 1st to 4th rows, inclusive of yoke patt 3 times. Cast off *loosely* knitwise. Complete other side of neck to match.

Sleeves

With $2\frac{1}{4}$mm (No 13) needles cast on 52 (52) sts. Work 10 rows in k1, p1 rib. Change to $2\frac{3}{4}$mm (No 12) needles.
Next row: K2, (inc in next st, k4) to end. 62 sts. Cont in st-st, beg p and inc 1 st each end of 2nd and every foll 4th row until there are 76 sts. Cont in st-st until work measures 9 (12)cm – $3\frac{1}{2}$ ($4\frac{1}{2}$)ins from beg, ending p.
  Now rep 26 rows of yoke patt as Back. Then rep 1st to 4th rows inclusive of yoke patt twice more. Cast off *loosely* knitwise.

Making up

Do not press. Sew top 4 rows of front over top 4 rows of back at each side edge. Sew cast-off edges of sleeves to sides of back and front for length of yoke patt. Join side and sleeve seams. Make 2 buttonhole loops each side of top front edge. Sew buttons to top of back to correspond. Press seams *lightly*.

Opposite: *Shetland Sweater (page 100) and Child's Aran Sweater (page 73)*

Guernsey Fingerless Gloves

A hard-wearing pair of gloves, knitted in stocking stitch with a band of Guernsey pattern above the welt, and with ribbed borders.

The pattern is in two sizes, to fit a standard woman's or man's hand. The gloves are knitted in navy 5-ply worsted wool.

Guernsey Fingerless Gloves

Opposite: *Child's Filey Guernsey (page 44) and Faroe Island Waistcoat (page 113)*

Materials: 2 (2) balls (50-gr) Poppleton Guernsey Wool 5-ply; two 2¾mm (No 12) needles.

Size: To fit average woman's (man's) hand.

Tension: 14 sts and 19 rows to 5cm – 2ins over stocking stitch on 2¾mm (No 12) needles.

Abbreviations: See page 116.

Right Hand

Cast on 44 (52) sts. Work 5cm – 2ins in k2, p2 rib.

Next row: Rib 2 (4), *inc in next st, rib 6 (5); rep from * to end. 50 (60) sts. Work 4 rows st-st, beg k.

Now work 16 rows of chart, rep 10-st patt rep 5 (6) times in each row, reading right side rows from right to left and wrong side rows from left to right.

K 1 row**.

Thumb Shaping: P25 (30), cast on 10 (11), TURN, k 20 (22), TURN. Work 11 rows st-st on these 20 (22) sts, beg p. Work 2 rows in k1, p1 rib. Cast off ribwise, leaving end for sewing. Join thumb seam.

With wrong side facing rejoin yarn and p 25 (30) to end.

Next row: K25 (30), pick up and k11 (12) sts from base of thumb, k15 (19) to end. 51 (61) sts. Work 19 rows in st-st, beg p.

*****1st Finger:** K33 (39), TURN, p15 (17), TURN. Work 10 rows st-st on these 15 (17) sts, beg k. Work 2 rows in k1, p1 rib, beg 2nd row p1. Cast off ribwise, leaving end for sewing. Join finger seam.

2nd Finger: With right side facing pick up and k 2 sts from base of 1st finger, k7 (8), TURN, p16 (18), TURN. Work 10 rows st-st on these 16 (18) sts, beg k. Work 2 rows in k1, p1 rib. Cast off ribwise, leaving end for sewing. Join finger seam.

3rd Finger: Work exactly as 2nd Finger, but pick up 2 sts from base of 2nd finger.

4th Finger: With right side facing pick up and k 2 sts from base of 3rd finger, k4 (6) to end, TURN, p10 (14). Work 6 rows st-st on these 10 (14) sts, beg k. Work 2 rows in k1, p1, rib. Cast off ribwise, leaving long end for sewing. Join side seam of glove. Press lightly, omitting ribbing.

Left Hand

As Right Hand to ***. P 1 row.

Thumb Shaping: K25 (30), cast on 10 (11), TURN, p20 (22), TURN. Work 10 rows st-st on these 20 (22) sts, beg k. Work 2 rows in k1, p1 rib. Cast off ribwise, leaving end for sewing. Join thumb seam.

With right side facing pick up and k11 (12) sts from base of thumb, k25 (30) to end, TURN, p 51 (61). Work 18 rows st-st, beg k.
Now complete as Right Hand from***.

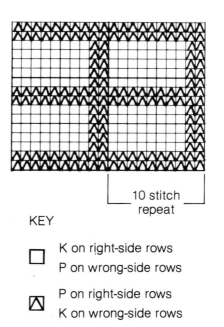

10 stitch repeat

KEY

☐ K on right-side rows
P on wrong-side rows

◺ P on right-side rows
K on wrong-side rows

Further Guernsey Pattern Panels

Four charts including more Guernsey patterns that can be incorporated into your own designs. Using 5-ply worsted wool on $2\frac{3}{4}$mm (No 12) needles or standard 4-ply on $3\frac{1}{4}$mm (No 10) needles, the tension should be 14 stitches and 18 rows to 5cm (2 inches) over all these patterns. Therefore by dividing the number of stitches required for the full width of your Guernsey by the number of stitches in each pattern panel or combination of panels, you can calculate how many repeats can be fitted into the width.

Herringbone, Rig and Furrow and Tree of Life

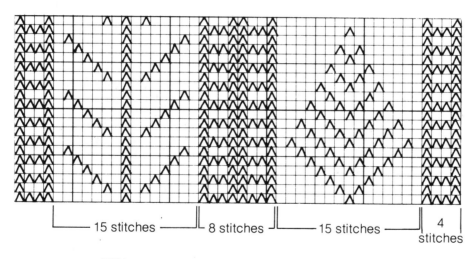

KEY

☐   K on right-side rows, P on wrong-side rows

◩   P on right-side rows, K on wrong-side rows

Triple Wave and Anchor

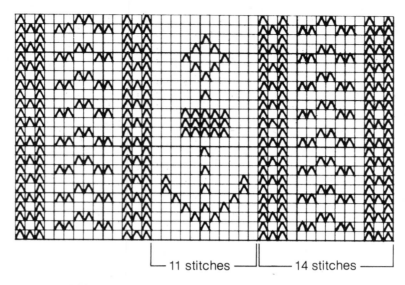

KEY

☐   K on right-side rows, P on wrong-side rows

◩   P on right-side rows, K on wrong-side rows

Ladder, Honeycomb and Net Mask

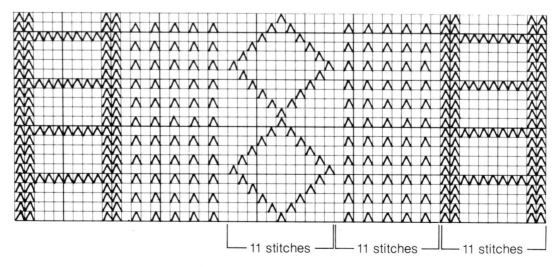

KEY

☐   K on right-side rows, P on wrong-side rows

◩   P on right-side rows, K on wrong-side rows

Marriage Lines, Sand and Diamond (Net Mask)

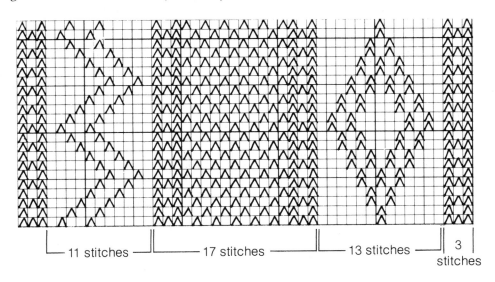

KEY

☐   K on right-side rows, P on wrong-side rows

◩   P on right-side rows, K on wrong-side rows

57

5
Arans

Across the entrance to Galway Bay, like three grey basking whales, lie the islands of Aran – Inisheer, Inishmaan and Inishmore. The largest and most north-westerly, Inishmore, is shaped like a knife with its tip pointing out into the Atlantic. The island is a great tilted slab of limestone, its south-western coast a sheer wall of cliffs against which the ocean continuously crashes, sucks and seethes.

Clinging to the top of the cliff at its highest point is one of the most impressive prehistoric structures in Europe, the fortress of Dun Aengus built by the Celts perhaps 2000 years ago. From Dun Aengus the land slopes down towards Galway Bay to the east in a series of gigantic steps along the bedding planes of the carboniferous limestone. At the south-eastern corner is Inishmaan's open mouth, the white sweeping curve of Kilronan Bay.

Inishmaan is grey and green, a landscape of limestone and ground-hugging vegetation. Ice sheets once scoured the island as clean as a cottage doorstep so that scarcely any soil remains to cover the protruding skeleton of rock. The people of Aran construct fields that look like fortresses. Huge stone walls surround their pocket-handkerchief sized plots and protect the crops from driving salt-laden winds. Seaweed and sand are hauled up from the beach to create soil where none exists. A tree is as rare here as on the Canadian tundra and peat for fuel is brought over from the mainland by boat.

The islands are most famous for their knitting which, until recently, remained remarkably localised, not spreading much into the mainland. In the last 20 years, however, it has become tremendously popular all over Britain. In Aran, the patterns used to be passed on within families from one generation to the next and not written down, but now they are more readily available. Unfortunately depopulation and tourism have undermined the folk art of Aran itself and much of the knitwear for sale on the islands is now specially imported to sell to the visitors.

The popularity of Aran-style knitwear is understandable. The thick, soft, creamy wool is knitted on fairly large needles into richly textured patterns that have an almost sculptural effect. These patterns in fact resemble the interlacing and bosses on the Irish stone crosses carved in the eighth and ninth centuries AD – motifs which originated on Celtic metalwork.

Manuscripts of the same period are covered with interlace patterns of staggering complexity. The *Book of Kells* also includes a bearded figure wearing a close-fitting garment covered in interlace pattern. It is not possible, however, to say that this

Inisheer, one of the islands of Aran

illustration definitely represents a knitted outfit. The origins of Aran knitwear like that of so many folk arts are unrecorded and unknown, though the designs obviously sprang from the mainstream of Celtic culture.

In Aran knitwear travelling stitches both plain and crossed, singly or in pairs or trebles, run across the surface of reversed stocking stitch. Cables are used extensively between other patterns. Some knitters decorate their work with bobbles, knitted in as the work progresses, though these can be overdone.

Like the fishing communities of Scotland and England the Aran knitters depicted the images and symbols of their everyday life – cables or fishing ropes, the diamond shapes of the fishing net mesh, zig-zag lightning and marriage lines. Characteristic of Aran in particular are trellis designs depicting their hard-won fields, and trinity stitch, a religious symbol dating back to the earliest days of Irish Christianity or even to the pagan trinities of the Celts.

Unlike Guernseys, Aran garments are not knitted in the round but are made in separate pieces which are sewn together. Aran-style wool is now widely available from commercial manufacturers and retailers.

Aran Polo Neck Sweater

An interesting Aran in which the back and front have horizontal bands of honeycomb cable, wide twisted chevrons, diamonds and trellis pattern. The shoulder bands and sleeves are worked in moss stitch and the polo collar and borders are in twisted rib.

The pattern is in two sizes only, due to the very wide pattern repeats; these will fit from 81–91cm (32–36 inch) to 96–107cm (38–42 inch) bust or chest.

Aran Polo Neck Sweater

Materials: 15 (18) balls (50-gr) Lister-Lee Aran Wool; two each 5mm (No 6) and 4½mm (No 7) needles; cable needle.

Measurements: To fit 81–91 (96–107)cm – 32–36 (38–42) in bust or chest; length, 61 (68)cm – 24 (27)ins; sleeve, 51 (56)cm – 20 (22)ins.

Tension: 17 sts and 30 rows to 10cm – 4ins over moss stitch on 5mm (No 6) needles.

Abbreviations: See page 116.

Aran Abbreviations:

c4b = cable 4 back – place next 2 sts on cable needle and leave at *back* of work, k2 then k2 from cable needle.

c4f = cable 4 front – place next 2 sts on cable needle and leave at *front* of work, k2 then k2 from cable needle.

t2r = twist 2 right – k 2nd st on left-hand needle then p first st and slip both sts off needle together.

t2l = twist 2 left – pull out 2nd st on left-hand needle to back of work and p then k first st and slip both sts off needle together.

tbl = through back of loop.

cr5 = cross 5 – place next 2 sts on cable needle and leave at *front* of work, k2, p1 then k2 from cable needle.

cr3r = cross 3 right – place next st on cable needle and leave at *back* of work, k2 then p1 from cable needle.

cr3l = cross 3 left – place next 2 sts on cable needle and leave at *front* of work, p1 then k2 from cable needle.

t2p = twist 2 purlwise – pull out 2nd st on left-hand needle to back of work and p then p first st and slip both sts off needle together.

Back

With 4½mm (No 7) needles cast on 81 (97) sts.
1st row: P1, (k1tbl, p1) to end.
2nd row: K1tbl, (p1, k1tbl) to end.
These 2 rows form *twisted rib.* Cont in twisted rib until work measures 11 (13)cm – 4½ (5)ins.
Change to 5mm (No 6) needles.
M-st row: K1, (p1, k1) to end. This row forms m-st on an odd number of sts. Cont to m-st until work measures 15 (19)cm – 6 (7½)ins from beg, ending with a right side row.

Next row: Inc in first st, *p4 (5), inc in next st; rep from * to end. 98 (114) sts.
Now work *cable patt* thus:
1st row: (right side). K1, (c4f, c4b) to last st, k1.
2nd row: P.
3rd row: K.
4th row: P.
5th row: K1, (c4b, c4f) to last st, k1.
6th row: P.
7th row: K.
8th row: P.
Now rep 1st to 5th rows again.
Next row: P2 tog, *p4 (5), p2 tog; rep from * to end. 81 (97) sts.
Work 6 rows in m-st, inc 4 sts evenly across last row *for 2nd size only.* 81 (101) sts.
Now work *chevron patt* thus:
1st row: (right side). P5, *(k1, p1) 5 times, k1, p9; rep from * to end, ending last rep with p5 instead of p9.
2nd row: K5, *(p1tbl, k1) 5 times, p1tbl, k9; rep from * to end, ending k5.
3rd row: P4, *(t2r) 3 times, p1, (t2l) 3 times, p7; rep from * to end, ending p4.
4th row: K4, *(p1tbl, k1) 3 times, k1, (k1, p1tbl) 3 times, k7; rep from * to end, ending k4.
5th row: P3, *(t2r) 3 times, p3, (t2l) 3 times, p5; rep from * to end, ending p3.
6th row: K3, *(p1tbl, k1) 3 times, k3, (k1, p1tbl) 3 times, k5; rep from * to end, ending k3.
7th row: P2, *(t2r) 3 times, p5, (t2l) 3 times, p3; rep from * to end, ending p2.
8th row: K2, *(p1tbl, k1) 3 times, k5, (k1, p1tbl) 3 times, k3: rep from * to end, ending k2.
9th row: P1, *(t2r) 3 times, p7, (t2l) 3 times, p1; rep from * to end.
10th row: K1, *(p1tbl, k1) 3 times, k7, (k1, p1tbl) 3 times, k1; rep from * to end.
11th row: P1, *(t2l) 3 times, p7, (t2r) 3 times, p1; rep from * to end.
12th row: As 8th row.
13th row: P2, *(t2l) 3 times, p5, (t2r) 3 times, p3; rep from * to end, ending p2.
14th row: As 6th row.
15th row: P3, *(t2l) 3 times, p3, (t2r) 3 times, p5; rep from * to end, ending p3.
16th row: As 4th row.
17th row: P4, *(t2l) 3 times, p1, (t2r) 3 times, p7; rep from * to end, ending p4.
18th row: As 2nd row.

19th row: As 1st row.

Work 6 rows in m-st, dec 4 sts evenly across last row *for 2nd size only*. 81 (97) sts.

Now work *diamond patt* thus:

1st row: (wrong side). K6, *p2, k1, p2, k11; rep from * to end, ending k6.

2nd row: P6, *cr5, p11; rep from * to end, ending p6.

3rd row: As 1st row.

4th row: P5, *cr3r, k1, cr3l, p9; rep from * to end, ending p5.

5th row: K5, *p2, k1, p1, k1,p2, k9; rep from * to end, ending k5.

6th row: P4, *cr3r, k1, p1, k1, cr3l, p7; rep from * to end, ending p4.

7th row: K4, *p2, k1, (p1, k1) twice, p2, k7; rep from * to end, ending k4.

8th row: P3, *cr3r, k1, (p1, k1) twice, cr3l, p5; rep from * to end, ending p3.

9th row: K3, *p2, k1, (p1, k1) 3 times, p2, k5; rep from * to end, ending k3.

10th row: P2, *cr3r, k1, (p1, k1) 3 times, cr3l, p3; rep from * to end, ending p2.

11th row: K2, *p2, k1, (p1, k1) 4 times, p2, k3; rep from * to end, ending k2.

12th row: P2, *cr3l, p1, (k1, p1) 3 times, cr3r, p3; rep from * to end, ending p2.

13th row: As 9th row.

14th row: P3, *cr3l, p1, (k1, p1) twice, cr3r; p5; rep from * to end, ending p3.

15th row: As 7th row.

16th row: P4, *cr3l, p1, k1, p1, cr3r, p7; rep from * to end, ending p4.

17th row: As 5th row.

18th row: P5, *cr3l, p1, cr3r, p9; rep from * to end, ending p5.

19th row: As 1st row.

20th row: As 2nd row.

Now work 6 rows in m-st, dec 1 st at end of last row *for 1st size* and inc 1 st at end of last row *for 2nd size*. 80 (98) sts.

Now work *trellis patt* thus:

1st row: (wrong side). K3, (t2p, k4) to end, ending k3.

2nd row: P2, (t2r, t2l, p2) to end.

3rd row: K2, (p1, k2) to end.

4th row: P1, (t2r, p2, t2l) to last st, p1.

5th row: K1, p1, (k4, t2p) to last 6 sts, k4, p1, k1.

6th row: P1, (t2l, p2, t2r) to last st, p1.

7th row: As 3rd row.

8th row: P2, (t2l, t2r, p2) to end.

Rep last 8 rows once more then 1st row again.

Work 1 row in m-st, inc 1 st at end of row *for 1st size* and dec 1 st at end of row *for 2nd size*. 81 (97) sts. Cont in m-st until work measures 61 (68)cm – 24 (27)ins from beg, ending with a wrong side row.

Shoulder Shaping: Cast off 26 (32) sts *loosely* in m-st at beg of next 2 rows. Leave 29 (33) sts on a spare needle.

Front

As Back until work measures 56 (63)cm – 22 (25)ins from beg, ending with a wrong side row.

Neck Shaping: *Next row:* M-st 30 (36), k2 tog, TURN. Work on these sts only. Dec 1 st at neck edge on next 5 rows. 26 (32) sts. Cont in m-st until work measures 61 (68)cm – 24 (27)ins from beg. Cast off *loosely* in m-st. Place centre 17 (21) sts on a st holder. Complete other side of neck to match.

Sleeves

With 4½mm (No 7) needles cast on 39 (43) sts. Work 10cm – 4ins in twisted rib as Back. Change to 5mm (No 6) needles and cont in m-st as Back, inc 1 st each end of every 6th row until there are 71 (79) sts. Cont straight in m-st until work measures 51 (56)cm – 20 (22)ins from beg. Cast off *loosely* in m-st.

Collar

Join right shoulder. With 4½mm (No 7) needles pick up and k 16 sts down left side of front neck, k sts from st holder, pick up and k 15 sts up right side of front neck then k sts from back neck. 77 (85) sts. Work 5cm – 2ins in twisted rib as Back. Change to 5mm (No 6) needles and cont in twisted rib until collar measures 15 (18)cm – 6 (7)ins from beg. Cast off *very loosely* in twisted rib.

Making up

Do not press. Join left shoulder and collar seam. Sew sleeve tops to sides of back and front, beg and ending 20 (23)cm – 8 (9)ins from shoulder seams. Join side and sleeve seams. Press seams lightly.

Aran Crew Neck Sweater

An intricately patterned Aran, with panels of diamond, branch and open cable travelling twisted stitches on a reversed stocking stitch background. At each side of the back and front there are moss stitch zig-zags on a stocking stitch background. The sleeves are mainly stocking stitch with a central diamond panel to match that on back and front.

The pattern is in two sizes, to fit from 86–94cm (34–37 inch) to 96–104cm (38–41 inch) bust or chest. (See illustration page 36.)

Materials: 15 (17) balls (50-gr) Aran Wool; two each 5mm (No 6) and 4½mm (No 7) needles; cable needle.

Measurements: To fit 86–94 (96–104)cm – 34–37 (38–41)in bust or chest; length, 63 (68)cm – 25 (27)ins; sleeve, 52 (56)cm – 20½ (22)ins.

Tension: 17 sts and 24 rows to 10cm – 4ins over stocking stitch on 5mm (No 6) needles.

Abbreviations: See page 116.

Aran Abbreviations:

t2r = twist 2 right – k 2nd st on left-hand needle then p first st and slip both sts off needle together.

t2l = twist 2 left – pull out 2nd st on left-hand needle to back of work and p then k first st and slip both sts off needle together.

t2p = twist 2 purlwise – pull out 2nd st on left-hand needle to back of work and p then p first st and slip both sts off needle together.

Back

With 4½mm (No 7) needles cast on 102 (112) sts. Work 8cm – 3ins in k1, p1 rib. Change to 5mm (No 6) needles.

Next row: (wrong side). P17 (22), k6, p3tbl, k6, (p1tbl, k2) 3 times, p1tbl, k6, p1tbl, k1, p2tbl, k1, p1tbl, k6, (p1tbl, k2) 3 times, p1tbl, k6, p3tbl, k6, p17 (22).

Now patt thus:

1st row: K14 (19), p1, k1, p1, *p5, t2r, k1tbl, t2l, p5*, (k1tbl, p2) 3 times, k1tbl, **p5, (t2r) twice, (t2l) twice, p5**, (k1tbl, p2) 3 times, k1tbl, rep from * to *, p1, k1, p1, k14 (19).

2nd row: P13 (18), (k1, p1) twice, *k5, p1tbl, (k1, p1tbl) twice, k5*, (p1tbl, k2) 3 times, p1tbl, **k5, (p1tbl, k1) twice, (k1, p1tbl) twice, k5**, (p1tbl, k2) 3 times, p1tbl, rep from * to *, (p1, k1) twice, p13 (18).

3rd row: K12 (17), (p1, k1) twice, k1, *p4, t2r, p1, k1tbl, p1, t2l, p4*, (k1tbl, p2) 3 times, k1tbl, **p4, (t2r) twice, p2, (t2l) twice, p4**, (k1tbl, p2) 3 times, k1tbl, rep from * to *, k1, (k1, p1) twice, k12 (17).

4th row: P11 (16), (k1, p1) twice, p2, *k4, p1tbl, (k2, p1tbl) twice, k4*, (p1tbl, k2) 3 times, p1tbl, **k4, (p1tbl, k1) twice, k2, (k1, p1tbl) twice, k4**, (p1tbl, k2) 3 times, p1tbl, rep from * to *, p2, (p1, k1) twice, p11 (16).

5th row: K10 (15), (p1, k1) twice, k3, *p3, t2r, p2, k1tbl, p2, t2l, p3*, (k1tbl, p2) 3 times, k1tbl, **p3, (t2r) twice, p4, (t2l) twice, p3**, (k1tbl, p2) 3 times, k1tbl, rep from * to *, k3, (k1, p1) twice, k10 (15).

6th row: P9 (14), (k1, p1) twice, p4, *k3, (p1tbl, k3) 3 times*, (p1tbl, k2) 3 times, p1tbl, **k3, (p1tbl, k1) twice, k4, (k1, p1tbl) twice, k3**, (p1tbl, k2) 3 times, p1tbl, rep from * to *, p4, (p1, k1) twice, p9 (14).

7th row: K8 (13), (p1, k1) twice, k5, *p2, t2r, p3, k1tbl, p3, t2l, p2*, k1tbl, p2, t2l, t2r, p2, k1tbl, **p2, (t2r) twice, k1tbl, p4, k1tbl, (t2l) twice, p2**, k1tbl, p2, t2l, t2r, p2, k1tbl, rep from * to *, k5, (k1, p1) twice, k8 (13).

8th row: P7 (12), k1, p1) twice, p6, *k2, (p1tbl, k4) twice, p1tbl, k2*, p1tbl, k3, t2p, k3, p1tbl, **k2, (p1tbl, k1) 3 times, k2, (k1, p1tbl) 3 times, k2**, p1tbl, k3, t2p, k3, p1tbl, rep from * to *, p6, (p1, k1) twice, p7 (12).

9th row: K6 (11), (p1, k1) twice, k7, *p1, t2r, p4, k1tbl, p4, t2l, p1*, k1tbl, p2, t2r, t2l, p2, k1tbl, **p1, (t2r) twice, p1, t2l, p2, t2r, p1, (t2l) twice, p1**, k1tbl, p2, t2r, t2l, p2, k1tbl, rep from * to *, k7, (k1, p1) twice, k6 (11).

10th row: P5 (10), (k1, p1) twice, p8, *k1, (p1tbl, k5) twice, p1tbl, k1*, (p1tbl, k2) 3 times, p1tbl, **(k1, p1tbl) twice, k3, p1tbl, k2, p1tbl, k3, (p1tbl, k1) twice**, (p1tbl, k2) 3 times, p1tbl, rep from * to *, p8, (p1, k1) twice, p5 (10).

11th row: K4 (9), (p1, k1) twice, k9, *t2r, p4, k3tbl, p4, t2l*, (k1tbl, p2) 3 times, k1tbl, **(t2r) twice, p3, t2l, t2r, p3, (t2l) twice**, (k1tbl, p2) 3 times, k1tbl, rep from * to *, k9, (k1, p1) twice, k4 (9).

12th row: P3 (8), (k1, p1) twice, p10, *p1tbl, k5, p3tbl, k5, p1tbl*, (p1tbl, k2) 3 times, p1tbl, **p1tbl, k1, p1tbl, k5, p2tbl, k5, p1tbl, k1, p1tbl**, (p1tbl, k2) 3 times, p1tbl, rep from * to *, p10, (p1, k1) twice, p3 (8).

13th row: K2 (7), (p1, k1) twice, k11, *p5, t2r, k1tbl, t2l, p5*, (k1tbl, p2) 3 times, k1tbl, **(t2l) twice, p3, t2r, t2l, p3, (t2r) twice**, (k1tbl, p2) 3 times, k1tbl, rep from * to *, k11 (k1, p1) twice, k2 (7).

14th row: P3 (8), (k1, p1) twice, p10, *k5, p1tbl, (k1, p1tbl) twice, k5*, (p1tbl, k2) 3 times, p1tbl, rep from ** to ** as 10th row, (p1tbl, k2) 3 times, p1tbl, rep from * to *, p10, (p1, k1) twice, p3 (8).

15th row: K4 (9), (p1, k1) twice, k9, *p4, t2r, p1, k1tbl, p1, t2l, p4*, (k1tbl, p2) 3 times, k1tbl, **p1, (t2l) twice, p1, t2r, p2, t2l, p1, (t2r) twice, p1**, (k1tbl, p2) 3 times, k1tbl, rep from * to *, k9, (k1, p1) twice, k4 (9).

16th row: P5 (10), (k1, p1) twice, p8, *k4, p1tbl, (k2, p1tbl) twice, k4*, (p1tbl, k2) 3 times, p1tbl, rep from ** to ** as 8th row, (p1tbl, k2) 3 times, p1tbl, rep from * to *, p8, (p1, k1) twice, p5 (10).

17th row: K6 (11), (p1, k1) twice, k7, *p3, t2r, p2, k1tbl, p2, t2l, p3*, (k1tbl, p2) 3 times, k1tbl, **p2, (t2l) twice, p6, (t2r) twice, p2**, (k1tbl, p2) 3 times, k1tbl, rep from * to *, k7, (k1, p1) twice, k6 (11).

18th row: P7 (12), (k1, p1) twice, p6, *k3, (p1tbl, k3) 3 times*, (p1tbl, k2) 3 times, p1tbl, rep from ** to ** as 6th row, (p1tbl, k2) 3 times, p1tbl, rep from * to *, p6, (p1, k1) twice, p7 (12).

19th row: K8 (13), (p1, k1) twice, k5, *p2, t2r, p3, k1tbl, p3, t2l, p2*, k1tbl, p2, t2l, t2r, p2, k1tbl, **p3, (t2l) twice, p4, (t2r) twice, p3**, k1tbl, p2, t2l, t2r, p2, k1tbl, rep from * to *, k5, (k1, p1) twice, k8 (13).

20th row: P9 (14), (k1, p1) twice, p4, *k2, (p1tbl, k4) twice, p1tbl, k2*, p1tbl, k3, t2p, k3, p1tbl, rep from ** to ** as 4th row, p1tbl, k3, t2p, k3, p1tbl, rep from * to *, p4, (p1, k1) twice, p9 (14).

21st row: K10 (15), (p1, k1) twice, k3, *p1, t2r, p4, k1tbl, p4, t2l, p1*, k1tbl, p2, t2r, t2l, p2, k1tbl, **p4, (t2l) twice, p2, (t2r) twice, p4**, k1tbl, p2, t2r, t2l, p2, k1tbl, rep from * to *, k3, (k1, p1) twice, k10 (15).

22nd row: P11 (16), (k1, p1) twice, p2, *k1, (p1tbl, k5) twice, p1tbl, k1*, (p1tbl, k2) 3 times, p1tbl, rep from ** to ** as 2nd row, (p1tbl, k2) 3 times, p1tbl, rep from * to *, p2, (p1, k1) twice, p11 (16).

23rd row: K12 (17), (p1, k1) twice, k1, *t2r, p4, k3tbl, p4, t2l*, (k1tbl, p2) 3 times, k1tbl, **p5, (t2l) twice, (t2r) twice, p5**, (k1tbl, p2) 3 times, k1tbl, rep from * to *, k1, (k1, p1) twice, k12 (17).

24th row: P13 (18), (k1, p1) twice, *p1tbl, k5, p3tbl, k5, p1tbl*, (p1tbl, k2) 3 times, p1tbl, **k6, p1tbl, k1, p2tbl, k1, p1tbl, k6**, (p1tbl, k2) 3 times, p1tbl, rep from * to *, (p1, k1) twice, p13 (18).

These 24 rows form patt.

Cont in patt until work measures 42 (46cm) – 16½ (18)ins from beg.

Armhole Shaping: Cast off 6 sts at beg of next 2 rows. 90 (100) sts. Cont in patt, keeping border patts correct for remaining sts, until work measures 63 (68)cm – 25 (27)ins from beg, ending with a wrong side row.

Shoulder Shaping: Cast off 29 (31) sts loosely at beg of next 2 rows. Leave 32 (38) sts on a spare needle.

Front

As Back until work measures 58 (63)cm − 23 (25)ins from beg, ending with a wrong side row.

Neck Shaping row: Patt 33 (35), k2 tog, TURN. Work on these sts only. Dec 1 st at neck edge on next 5 rows. 29 (31) sts. Work 6 rows straight. Cast off *loosely*. Place centre 20 (26) sts on a st holder. Complete other side of neck to match.

Sleeves

With 4½mm (No 7) needles cast on 44 (48) sts. Work 8cm − 3ins in k1, p1 rib. Change to 5mm (No 6) needles.

Next row: (wrong side). P9 (11), (k1, p1tbl) twice, k6, p1tbl, k1, p2tbl, k1, p1tbl, k6, (p1tbl, k1) twice, p9 (11).
Now patt thus:

1st row: K9 (11), (p1, k1tbl) twice, rep from ** to ** as 1st patt row of Back, (k1tbl, p1) twice, k9 (11).

2nd row: P9 (11), (k1, p1tbl) twice, rep from ** to ** as 2nd patt row, (p1tbl, k1) twice, p9 (11).

Cont in this way, working centre panel of 18 sts as Back patt from ** to ** with 4 rib sts each side of panel and side edges in st-st, *at same time* inc 1 st each end of every 4th row until there are 86 (92) sts, working extra sts into st-st. Cont straight with centre patt as before until work measures 56 (60)cm − 22 (23½)ins from beg. Cast off *loosely*.

Neckband

Join right shoulder. With 4½mm (No 7) needles pick up and k 12 sts down left side of front neck, k sts from st holder, pick up and k 12 sts up right side of front neck then k sts from back neck. 76 (88) sts. Work 18 rows in k1, p1 rib. Cast off *very loosely* ribwise.

Making up

Press lightly, omitting ribbing. Join left shoulder and neckband seam. Fold neckband in half to wrong side and slip-st down loosely. Set in sleeves, joining 4cm − 1½ins of sides of sleeves to cast-off armhole sts. Join side and sleeve seams. Press seams.

Aran Cardigan

A woman's cardigan knitted in a combination of diamond, cable and trinity stitch patterns. The neckband, front bands and cuffs are worked in rib, but the lower border is in trinity stitch which makes a firm and unusual edging. The sleeves have a repeat of the diamond and cable designs of the back and fronts, with reversed stocking stitch borders.

The pattern is in three sizes, to fit from 84cm (33 inch) to 104cm (41 inch) bust. (See illustration page 105.)

Materials: 16 (17:19) balls (50-gr) Lister-Lee Aran Wool; two each 5mm (No 6), 4½mm (No 7) and 3¾mm (No 9) needles; cable needle; 8 buttons.

Measurements: To fit 84–89 (91–96:99–104)cm – 33–35 (36–38:39–41)in bust; length, 63 (65:66)cm – 25 (25½:26)ins; sleeve, 46cm – 18ins.

Tension: 17 sts and 24 rows to 10cm – 4ins over stocking stitch on 5mm (No 6) needles. 16 sts and 18 rows to 8cm – 3ins over trinity stitch on 5mm (No 6) needles.

Abbreviations: See page 116.

Aran Abbreviations:

cr5 = cross 5 – place next 2 sts on cable needle and leave at *front* of work, k2, p1 then k2 from cable needle.

cr3r = cross 3 right – place next st on cable needle and leave at *back* of work, k2 then p1 from cable needle.

cr3l = cross 3 left – place next 2 sts on cable needle and leave at *front* of work, p1 then k2 from cable needle.

c4b = cable 4 back – place next 2 sts on cable needle and leave at *back* of work, k2 then k2 from cable needle.

c4f = cable 4 front – place next 2 sts on cable needle and leave at *front* of work, k2 then k2 from cable needle.

Back

With 4½mm (No 7) needles cast on 102 (110:118) sts. K 1 row.

Now work *trinity st* thus:

1st row: (right side). P.

2nd row: K1, *work: (k1, p1, k1) all in next st, p3 tog*; rep from * to * to last st, k1.

3rd row: P.

4th row: K1, *p3 tog, work: (k1, p1, k1) all in next st*; rep from * to * to last st, k1.

These 4 rows form trinity st.

Work 12 rows more in trinity st, inc 1 st each end of last row. 104 (112:120) sts. Change to 5mm (No 6) needles and patt thus:

1st row: P6 (10:14), **k4, p1, k4, p6, cr5, p6, k4, p1, k4**, p22, rep from ** to **, p6 (10:14).

2nd row: K1, rep from * to * as 2nd row of trinity st once (twice: 3 times), k1, **p4, k1, p4, k6, p2, k1, p2, k6, p4, k1, p4**, k1, rep from * to * as 2nd row of trinity st 5 times, k1, rep from ** to **, k1, rep from * to * as 2nd row of trinity st once (twice: 3 times), k1.

3rd row: P6 (10:14), **k4, p1, k4, p5, cr3r, k1, cr3l, p5, k4, p1, k4**, p22, rep from ** to **, p6 (10:14).

4th row: K1, rep from * to * as 4th row of trinity st once (twice: 3 times), k1, **p4, k1, p4, k5, p2, k1, p1, k1, p2, k5, p4, k1, p4**, k1, rep from * to * as 4th row of trinity st 5 times, k1 rep from ** to **, k1, rep from * to * as 4th row of trinity st once (twice: 3 times), k1.

These 4 rows form trinity st for first and last 6 (10:14) st and centre 22 sts and will now be referred to as 'patt' throughout.

5th row: Patt 6 (10:14), **c4f, p1, c4b, p4, cr3r, k1, p1, k1, cr3l, p4, c4b, p1, c4f**, patt 22, rep from ** to **, patt 6 (10:14).

6th row: Patt 6 (10:14), **p4, k1, p4, k4, p2, k1, (p1, k1) twice, p2, k4, p4, k1, p4**, patt 22, rep from ** to **, patt 6 (10:14).

7th row: Patt 6 (10:14), **k4, p1, k4, p3, cr3r, k1, (p1, k1) twice, cr3l, p3, k4, p1, k4**, patt 22, rep from ** to **, patt 6 (10:14).

8th row: Patt 6 (10:14), **p4, k1, p4, k3, p2, k1, (p1, k1) 3 times, p2, k3, p4, k1, p4**, patt 22, rep from ** to **, patt 6 (10:14).

9th row: Patt 6 (10:14), **k4, p1, k4, p2, cr3r, k1, (p1, k1) 3 times, cr3l, p2, k4, p1, k4**, patt 22, rep from ** to **, patt 6 (10:14).

10th row: Patt 6 (10:14), **p4, k1, p4, k2, p2, k1, (p1, k1) 4 times, p2, k2, p4, k1, p4**, patt 22, rep from ** to **, patt 6 (10:14).

11th row: Patt 6 (10:14), **c4f, p1, c4b, p2, cr3l, p1, (k1, p1) 3 times, cr3r, p2, c4b, p1, c4f**, patt 22, rep from ** to **, patt 6 (10:14).

12th row: As 8th row.

13th row: Patt 6 (10:14), **k4, p1, k4, p3, cr3l, p1, (k1, p1) twice, cr3r, p3, k4, p1, k4**, patt 22, rep from ** to **, patt 6 (10:14).

14th row: As 6th row.

15th row: Patt 6 (10:14), **k4, p1, k4, p4, cr3l, p1, k1, p1, cr3r, p4, k4, p1, k4**, patt 22, rep from ** to **, patt 6 (10:14).

16th row: As 4th row.

17th row: Patt 6 (10:14). **c4f, p1, c4b, p5, cr3l, p1, cr3r, p5, c4b, p1, c4f**, patt 22, rep from ** to **, patt 6 (10:14).

18th row: As 2nd row.

These 18 rows form patt for *diamond* and *cable* panels. Cont in patt, keeping 4-row trinity st patt in line, until work measures 43cm – 17ins from beg.

Armhole Shaping: Keeping patt correct, cast off 4 (3:7) sts at beg of next 2 rows then dec 1 st each end of next 6 rows. 84 (94:94) sts. Cont in patt as set until work measures 63 (65:66)cm – 25 (25½:26)ins from beg, ending with a wrong side row.

Shoulder Shaping: Cast off 27 (32:32) sts *loosely* at beg of next 2 rows. Leave 30 sts on spare needle.

Right Front

With 4½mm (No 7) needles cast on 50 (54:58) sts. K 1 row then work 16 rows in trinity st as Back, inc 1 st at end of last row. 51 (55:59) sts***. Change to 5mm (No 6) needles and patt thus:

1st row: P10, rep from ** to ** as 1st row of Back patt, p6 (10:14).

2nd row: K1, rep from * to * as 2nd row of trinity st once (twice: 3 times), k1, rep from ** to ** as 2nd row of Back patt, k1, rep from * to * as 2nd row of trinity st twice, k1.

Placing diamond and cable panel between 10 trinity sts at front edge and 6 (10:14) trinity sts at side edge, cont in patt as Back until work measures 43cm – 17ins from beg, ending with a right side row.

Armhole Shaping: Cast off 4 (3:7) sts at beg of next row then dec 1 st at armhole edge on next 6 rows. 41 (46:46) sts. Cont in patt until work measures 56 (57:58)cm – 22 (22½:23)ins from beg, ending with a wrong side row.

Neck Shaping: Cast off 8 sts at beg of next row then dec 1 st at neck edge on next 6 rows. 27 (32:32) sts. Cont straight until work measures 63 (65:66)cm – 25 (25½:26)ins from beg. Cast off *loosely*.

Left Front

As Right Front to ***. Change to 5mm (No 6) needles and patt thus:

1st row: P6 (10:14), rep from ** to ** as 1st row of Back patt, p10.

Reversing trinity st borders in this way, complete to match Right Front, also reversing armhole and neck shapings.

Sleeves

With 4½mm (No 7) needles cast on 49 (51:53) sts. Work 6cm – 2½ins in k1, p1 rib, beg 2nd row p1. Change to 5mm (No 6) needles and patt thus:

1st row: P7 (8:9), rep from ** to ** as 1st row of Back patt, p7 (8:9).

2nd row: K7 (8:9), rep from ** to ** as 2nd row of back patt, k7 (8:9).

Placing diamond and cable panel at centre in this way, work borders in reversed st-st, inc 1 st each end of next and every foll 8th row, working extra sts into reversed st-st, until there are

65 (71:75) sts. Cont straight until work measures 46cm – 18ins from beg.

Top Shaping: Cast off 4 (3:7) sts at beg of next 2 rows then dec 1 st each end of every alt row until 31 (31:31) sts remain. Dec 1 st each end of next 6 rows. Cast off remaining 19 sts loosely.

Front Bands and Neckband

Join shoulders. With 3¾mm (No 9) needles cast on 10 sts for left front band.
1st row: (right side). K2, (p1, k1) 4 times.
Rep this row until band measures 56 (57:58)cm – 22 (22½:23)ins, slightly stretched and ending with a wrong side row. Break yarn and leave sts on safety pin.

With 3¾mm (No 9) needles cast on 10 sts for right front band. Work 6 rows in rib as left front band.

Buttonhole row: Rib 4, cast off 3, rib 3.
Next row: Rib 3, cast on 3, rib 4.
Cont in rib as before, making 6 more buttonholes 8cm – 3ins apart (measure from base of previous buttonhole with work slightly stretched). After 7th buttonhole cont in rib until band is same length as left front band, ending with a wrong side row.
Next row: Rib 10, pick up and k 26 sts around right side of front neck, k sts from back neck, pick up and k 26 sts around left side of front neck then rib 10 sts of left front band. 102 sts.
Work 9 rows in rib, making 8th buttonhole as before, at beg of 4th row. Cast off ribwise.

Making up

Do not press. Join side and sleeve seams. Set in sleeves. Sew on front bands. Press seams lightly. Sew on buttons.

Aran Jacket

A woman's jacket worked in trinity stitch with ribbed borders and collar. The jacket has straight sides and straight-topped sleeves to give an easy-fitting drop shoulder line. Trinity stitch is so called because the pattern is made by working three into one and then one into three. In England it is also known as blackberry stitch and is used widely in knitting patterns apart from Aran designs.

The pattern is in three sizes, to fit from 84cm (33 inch) to 104cm (41 inch) bust.

Aran Jacket

Materials: 16 (18:19) balls (50-gr) Aran Wool; two each 5mm (No 6) and 3¾mm (No 9) needles; 6 buttons.

Measurements: To fit 84–89 (91–96:99–104)cm – 33–35 (36–38:39–41)in bust; length, 56 (58:61)cm – 22 (23:24)ins; sleeve, 50cm – 19¾ins.

Tension: 16 sts and 18 rows to 8cm – 3ins over trinity stitch on 5mm (No 6) needles.

Abbreviations: See page 116.

Back

With 3¾mm (No 9) needles cast on 86 (92:100) sts. Work 12cm – 4¾ins in k1, p1 rib.
Next row: Rib 6 (2:10), *inc in next st, rib 4; rep from * to end. 102 (110:118) sts. Change to 5mm (No 6) needles and work *trinity st* thus:
1st row: (right side). P.
2nd row: K1, *work: (k1, p1, k1) all in next st, p3 tog; rep from * to last st, k1.
3rd row: P.
4th row: K1, *p3 tog, work: (k1, p1, k1) all in next st; rep from * to last st, k1. These 4 rows form trinity st.
Cont in trinity st until work measures 56 (58:61)cm – 22 (23:24)ins from beg, ending with a 2nd or 4th row.

Shoulder Shaping: Cast off 34 (38:42) sts loosely at beg of next 2 rows. Leave 34 sts on spare needle.

Right Front

With 3¾mm (No 9) needles cast on 42 (46:50) sts. Work 12cm – 4¾ins in k1, p1 rib.
Next row: Rib 2 (6:10), *inc in next st, rib 4; rep from * to end. 50 (54:58) sts.
Change to 5mm (No 6) needles and work in trinity st as Back until work measures 49 (52:54)cm – 19½ (20½:21½)ins from beg, ending with a 2nd or 4th patt row.

Neck Shaping: Keeping patt correct, cast off 8 sts at beg of next row then dec 1 st at neck edge on next 8 rows. 34 (38:42) sts. Cont until work measures 56 (58:61)cm – 22 (23:24)ins from beg. Cast off loosely.

Left Front

As Right Front, reversing neck shaping.

Sleeves

With 3¾mm (No 9) needles cast on 44 (44:44) sts. Work 12cm – 4¾ins in k1, p1 rib.
Next row: Rib 2, *inc in next st, rib 2; rep from * to end. 58 sts.
Change to 5mm (No 6) needles and work in trinity st as Back, inc 1 st each end of every 4th row until there are 90 (98:104) sts, working extra sts into patt when there are 4 extra sts at each side to make a patt rep. Cont straight until work measures 50cm – 19¾ins from beg, ending with a 2nd or 4th row. Cast off *loosely*.

Front Bands and Collar

Join shoulders. With 3¾mm (No 9) needles cast on 8 sts for left front band. Work 49 (52:54)cm – 19½ (20½:21½)ins in k1, p1 rib, slightly stretched. Leave sts on a safety pin.
With 3¾mm (No 9) needles cast on 8 sts for right front band. Work 4 rows in k1, p1 rib.

Buttonhole row: Rib 3, cast off 3, rib 2.
Next row: Rib 2, cast on 3, rib 3.
Cont in rib, making 5 more buttonholes 9 (9½:10)cm – 3½ (3¾:4)ins apart (measure from base of previous buttonhole with work slightly stretched). Work 2 rows more after 6th buttonhole is completed.
Next row: Rib 8, pick up and k 24 sts around right side of front neck, k sts from back neck, pick up and k 24 sts around left side of front neck then rib sts of left front band. 98 sts.
Work 12cm – 4¾ins in k1, p1 rib. Cast off loosely ribwise.

Making up

Do not press. Sew cast-off edges of sleeves to sides of back and fronts, beg and ending 20 (22:23)cm – 8 (8½:9)ins from shoulder seams. Join side and sleeve seams. Sew on front bands. Press seams lightly. Sew on buttons.

Aran Waistcoat

It is not widely known that there are a few openwork Aran stitches in addition to the more common cables, diamonds and bobbles. This woman's or girl's waistcoat is knitted in an all-over openwork Aran pattern and has double crochet borders. It is worked in one piece with the crochet borders added afterwards.

The pattern is in six sizes, to fit from 61cm (24 inch) to 104cm (41 inch) chest or bust.

Aran Waistcoat

Materials: 4 (5:6:7:8:9) balls (50-gr) Lister-Lee Aran Wool; two 5mm (No 6) needles; 4.50mm crochet hook.

Measurements: To fit 61–66 (68–73:76–81: 84–89:91–96:99–104)cm – 24–26 (27–29:30–32: 33–35: 36–38: 39–41)in chest or bust; length, 43 (48:53:58:63:68)cm – 17 (19:21:23:25:27)ins.

Tension: On 5mm (No 6) needles: 1 patt rep (12 sts) to 8cm – 3 ins; 13 rows to 5cm – 2ins.

Abbreviations: See page 116.

To make

With 5mm (No 6) needles cast on 111 (123:135: 147:159:171) sts. K 2 rows. Now patt thus:

1st row: (right side). P5, (k5, p7) to last 10 sts, k5, p5.

2nd and every alternate row: P.

3rd row: P3, p2 tog, (k2, yfd, k1, yfd, k2, p2, p3 tog, p2) to last 10 sts, k2, yfd, k1, yfd, k2, p2 tog, p3.

5th row: P2, p2 tog, (k2, yfd, k3, yfd, k2, p1, p3 tog, p1) to last 11 sts, k2, yfd, k3, yfd, k2, p2 tog, p2.

7th row: P1, p2 tog, (k2, yfd, k5, yfd, k2, p3 tog) to last 12 sts, k2, yfd, k5, yfd, k2, p2 tog, p1.

8th row: P.

These 8 rows form patt. Cont in patt until 9 (10: 11:12:13:14) patts are completed from beg, but end last rep with a 7th patt row.

Armhole Dividing row: (wrong side). P21 (27:27:33:33:39), cast off 15 (9:9:15:15:9) sts

purlwise for left armhole, p39 (51:63:51:63:75), cast off 15 (9:9:15:15:9) sts purlwise for right armhole, p21 (27:27:33:33:39) to end. Work on last set of sts for **Right Front.** Cont in patt as set until 12 (13:14:15:17:19) patts have been completed from beg.

Neck Shaping: Cast off 2 (8:8:8:8:8) sts at beg of next row then dec 1 st at neck edge on next 4 rows. 15 (15:15:21:21:27) sts. Cont straight until 14 (15:17:18:20:22) patts are completed from beg. Cast off *loosely.*

Back: Rejoin yarn to centre set of sts and work in patt until 14 (15:17:18:20:22) patts are completed from beg. Cast off *loosely.*

Left Front: Rejoin yarn to remaining sts and work to match Right Front, but shape neck after 7th row of 12th (13th:14th:15th:17th: 19th) patt, thus reversing neck shaping.

Making up and Borders

Press lightly. Join shoulders. With 4.50mm hook work in double crochet up right front edge, around neck and down left front edge, TURN. Work a 2nd row of double crochet. Fasten off. With 4.50mm hook work 1 row double crochet around armhole edge beg at centre of armhole cast-off sts, TURN. Work 2nd row in double crochet. Fasten off and join sides of border. Work 2nd armhole border to match. Press seams and borders lightly.

Child's Aran Sweater

A classic crew neck Aran, with a large centre panel of diamond trellis on the back and front, and cable panels at each side and at centre of sleeves. The remainder of the sweater is worked in reversed stocking stitch with ribbed borders.

The pattern is in five sizes, to fit 61cm (24 inch) to 81cm (32 inch) chest. (See illustration page 52.)

Materials: 7 (9:11:13:15) balls (50-gr) Lister-Lee Aran Wool; two each 5mm (No 6) and 4½mm (No 7) needles; cable needle.

Measurements: To fit 61 (66:71:76:81)cm – 24 (26:28:30:32)in chest; length, 44 (48:52:56:60)cm – 17½ (19:20½:22:23½)ins; sleeve, 30 (34:38:42:46)cm – 12 (13½:15:16½:18)ins.

Tension: 17 sts and 24 rows to 10cm – 4ins over stocking stitch on 5mm (No 6) needles.

Abbreviations: See page 116.

Aran Abbreviations:

cr3r = cross 3 right – place next st on cable needle and leave at **back** of work, k2 then p1 from cable needle.

cr3l = cross 3 left – place next 2 sts on cable needle and leave at *front* of work, p1 then k2 from cable needle.

cr4p = cross 4 purlwise – place next 2 sts on cable needle and leave at *front* of work, p2 then p2 from cable needle.

cab3r = cable 3 right – place next 2 sts on cable needle and leave at *back* of work, k1 then k2 from cable needle.

cab3l = cable 3 left – place next st on cable needle and leave at *front* of work, k2 then k1 from cable needle.

Back

With 4½mm (No 7) needles cast on 62 (66:70:76:80) sts. Work 5cm – 2ins in k1, p1 rib. Change to 5mm (No 6) needles.

Next row: P8 (10:12:15:17), k7, p8, (k4, p8) twice, k7, p8 (10:12:15:17).

Next row: K8 (10:12:15:17), p7, k8, (p4tbl, k8) twice, p7, k8 (10:12:15:17).

Now patt thus:

1st row: (right side). P8 (10:12:15:17), cab3r, k1, cab3l, p7, (cr3r, cr3l, p6) twice, p1, cab3r, k1, cab3l, p8 (10:12:15:17).

2nd row: K8 (10:12:15:17), p7, k7 (p2tbl, k2, p2tbl, k6) twice, k1, p7, k8 (10:12:15:17).

3rd row: P8 (10:12:15:17), k7, p6, (cr3r, p2, cr3l, p4) twice, p2, k7, p8 (10:12:15:17).

4th row: K8 (10:12:15:17), p7, k6, (p2tbl, k4) 4 times, k2, p7, k8 (10:12:15:17). These 4 rows establish patt for 7-st cable panels and outer side panels which are rep throughout Back and Front, and will be referred to as 'patt 15 (17:19:22:24)'.

5th row: Patt 15 (17:19:22:24), p5, (cr3r, p4, cr3l, p2) twice, p3, patt to end.

6th row: Patt 15 (17:19:22:24), k5, (p2tbl, k6, p2tbl, k2) twice, k3, patt to end.

7th row: Patt 15 (17:19:22:24), p4, (cr3r, p6, cr3l) twice, p4, patt to end.

8th row: Patt 15 (17:19:22:24), k4, p2tbl, k8, cr4p, k8, p2tbl, k4, patt to end.

9th row: Patt 15 (17:19:22:24), p4, (cr3l, p6, cr3r) twice, p4, patt to end.

10th row: As 6th row.

11th row: Patt 15 (17:19:22:24), p5, (cr3l, p4, cr3r, p2) twice, p3, patt to end.

12th row: As 4th row.

13th row: Patt 15 (17:19:22:24), p6, (cr3l, p2, cr3r, p4) twice, p2, patt to end.

14th row: As 2nd row.

15th row: Patt 15 (17:19:22:24), p7, (cr3l, cr3r, p6) twice, p1, patt to end.

16th row: Patt 15 (17:19:22:24), k8, (cr4p, k8) twice, patt to end.

These 16 rows form patt for centre trellis patt. Cont in patt until work measures 29(32:34:37:40)cm − 11½ (12½:13½:14½:15½)ins from beg.

Armhole Shaping: Cast off 5 sts at beg of next 2 rows. 52 (56:60:66:70) sts. Cont with patt panels as before until work measures 44 (48:52:56:60)cm − 17½ (19:20½:22:23½)ins from beg, ending with a wrong side row.

Shoulder Shaping: Cast off 13 (14:16:18:20) sts *loosely* at beg of next 2 rows. Leave 26 (28:28:30:30) sts on spare needle.

Front

As Back until work measures 40 (44:48:52:56)cm − 16 (17½:19:20½:22)ins from beg, ending with a wrong side row.

Neck Shaping: *Next row:* Patt 15 (16:18:20:22), k2 tog, TURN. Work on these sts only. Dec 1 st at neck edge on next 3 rows. 13 (14:16:18:20) sts. Work 6 rows straight. Cast off loosely. Place centre 18 (20:20:22:22) sts on a st holder. Complete other side of neck to match.

Sleeves

With 4½mm (No 7) needles cast on 29 (31:33:35:37) sts. Work 6cm − 2½ins in k1, p1 rib, beg

2nd row p1. Change to 5mm (No 6) needles and patt thus:

1st row: (right side). P11 (12:13:14:15), k7, p11 (12:13:14:15).

2nd row: K11 (12:13:14:15), p7, k11 (12:13:14:15).

3rd row: P11 (12:13:14:15), cab3r, k1, cab3l, p11 (12:13:14:15).

4th row: As 2nd row.

These 4 rows form patt for centre 7-st cable panel. Cont in patt, inc 1 st each end of next and every following 4th row until there are 53 (59:63:67:71) sts, working extra sts into reversed st-st. Cont straight until work measures 33 (37:41:45:49)cm − 13¼ (14¾:16¼:17¾:19¼)ins from beg. Cast off *loosely*.

Neckband

Join right shoulder. With 4½mm (No 7) needles pick up and k 11 sts down left side of front neck, k sts from st holder, pick up and k 11 sts up right side of front neck, then k sts from back neck. 66 (70:70:74:74) sts. Work 6 rows in k1, p1 rib. Cast off *very loosely* ribwise.

Making up

Do not press. Join left shoulder and neckband seam. Set in sleeves, joining 3cm − 1¼ins of sides of sleeves to cast-off 5 armhole sts. Join side and sleeve seams. Press seams and sweater lightly.

6
Colour Knitting

In contrast to the textured patterns of Guernseys and Arans, the patterns in the Fair Isle, Shetland and Faroe Island traditions are produced by using a variety of colours. In colour knitting the garments are worked in a plain stocking stitch, using a fine but loosely spun wool (Shetland). While no more than two colours are used in any one row, these two colours may be changed any number of times, allowing intricate patterns to be built up.

Probably the best known colour knitting of all is that from Fair Isle, a tiny island half way between Orkney and Shetland. Fair Isle patterns are always knitted on a

Transporting sheep in Fair Isle

background of natural fleece colours – white, grey, cream or brown. The rich, multi-coloured effect is built up by continually changing both the background and pattern colours.

In a strictly traditional Fair Isle, the sequence of patterning should change all the way up the garment. A broad pattern in a multiplicity of colours is generally followed by a narrow pattern in only two or three colours. Before the introduction of modern dyes, Shetland wool was restricted in colour to blues, reds and yellows in addition to the natural shades, but in the last few decades the range has widened enormously.

Folk tradition has it that Fair Isle designs were first copied from the garments of Spanish sailors wrecked after the Armada. The accuracy of this theory is uncertain, but the designs do bear a close resemblance to the rich patterns of Catholic Europe. The names of some patterns – Armada cross, sacred heart, star of Bethlehem – seem to reflect this origin, although the date at which they were given is unknown.

The symbolism in the Fair Isle garments is best seen in the so-called Robes of Glory. These were knitted by the older women for their grandsons to wear when they reached adolescence. In a typical example, the pattern representing the water of life is followed by the seed of life, which is nurtured into the flower of life. The anchor of hope is accompanied by the star of Bethlehem to guide the boy on his way, and the crown of glory symbolises the reward for a life well led.

By contrast, the hand-knitting tradition of neighbouring Shetland owes much to Scandinavian influences. Shetland designs are worked in a variety of natural colours – beiges, creams, greys and browns, the ground shade remaining constant. A bright colour is sometimes introduced to highlight the pattern. There are two basic types of Shetland design. One consists of an all-over pattern often worked in alternating diamonds. The other type has bands of coloured patterning, with a dark pattern on a light ground alternating with a light pattern on a dark ground.

One hundred and eighty miles north west of Shetland and half way to Iceland, the Faroe Islands, belonging to Denmark, also maintain the basically Scandinavian knitting tradition. Their colours and patterns are bright and bold, in contrast to the more subdued and subtle shades used in Shetland. The background colour again remains constant but the body of the garment is seeded with splashes of colour. Single or grouped stitches form an all-over pattern on the uniform background, while the yokes are highly patterned with vivid geometric designs.

Opposite: *The Faroe Islands support a little crofting and fishing, but their main livelihood stems from knitting*

Fair Isle Waistcoat

An excellent example of true Fair Isle knitting at its most intricate. The light beige background is carried through the whole design, and on to this seven other colours are introduced in four different patterns. Shades of brown and green are combined with white and purple. The borders are in rib and the front band can be reversed as it is worked separately and sewn on afterwards.

The pattern is in one size only because of the varying widths of the pattern repeats. It will fit a man with 97–102cm (38–40 inch) chest as shown, or it can be worn by a woman with 86–91cm (34–36 inch) bust as a slightly looser style. The waistcoat is knitted in Shetland 2-ply Jumper Weight wool, which is equivalent to standard 4-ply. (See illustration page 105.)

Materials: Of Shetland Wool 2-ply Jumper Weight (4-ply equivalent): 4 hanks (2-oz) Light Beige (shade 202), 2 hanks (2-oz) Dark Brown (5), 2 hanks (1-oz) White (1), 1 hank (1-oz) each Dark Green (47), Mid Brown (4), Ginger (45), Purple (20) and Light Green (25); two each 3¼mm (No 10) and 2¾mm (No 12) needles; 5 buttons.

Measurements: To fit 86–91 cm – 34–36in bust loosely; or 97–102cm – 38–40in chest slimfit; length, 61cm – 24ins.

Tension: 14 sts and 15 rows to 5cm – 2ins over Fair Isle on 3¼mm (No 10) needles.

Abbreviations: See page 116.

Colour Abbreviation: LB = Light Beige.

Back

With 2¾mm (No 12) needles and LB cast on 133 sts. Work 8cm – 3ins in k1, p1 rib, beg 2nd row p1. Change to 3¼mm (No 10) needles. Work 2 rows in st-st, beg k.
*Still working in st-st work 5 rows patt from chart A, reading k rows from right to left and p rows from left to right and working 1 st beyond dotted line *at end of k rows and beg of p rows only.*
Work 2 rows in LB, beg p.
Now work 29 rows patt from chart B, beg with a p row and working 5 sts beyond dotted line *at beg of p rows and end of k rows only.*
Work 2 rows in LB, beg k.
**Now work 5 rows from chart C, beg with a k row and reading chart as for chart A.
Work 2 rows LB, beg p.
Now work 20 rows from chart D, beg with a p row and reading chart as for chart A.
Work 2 rows LB, beg p.
Now rep 5 rows from chart C again, beg p.
Work 2 rows LB, beg k**. The 74 rows from * form the complete Fair Isle patt. Beg at * again and work until 12th row of chart B is completed.

Armhole Shaping: Keeping chart patt correct, cast off 8 sts at beg of next 2 rows then dec 1 st each end of next 12 rows. 93 sts. Keeping chart patts in line, cont until 2nd set of 74 rows is completed then rep 5 rows of chart A again. Cont in LB only. P 1 row.

Shoulder Shaping: Cast off 30 sts loosely at beg of next 2 rows. Cast off remaining 33 sts loosely.

CHART D

20

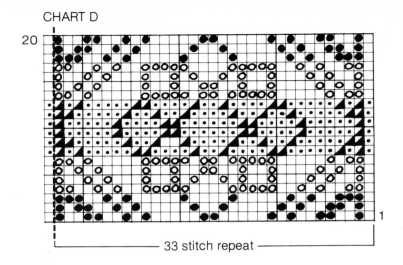

1

└── 33 stitch repeat ──┘

CHART C

5

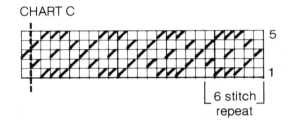

1

└─ 6 stitch ─┘
repeat

CHART B

29

12

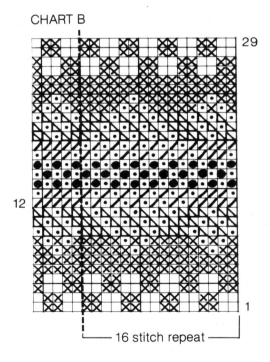

1

└── 16 stitch repeat ──┘

KEY

☐ Light beige

◩ Dark green

⊠ Dark brown

⊡ White

◨ Mid brown

◪ Ginger

⊙ Purple

⊡ Light green

CHART A

5

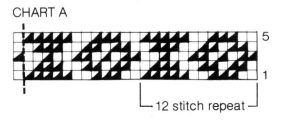

1

└─ 12 stitch repeat ─┘

Right Front

With 2¾mm (No 12) needles and LB cast on 67 sts. Work 8cm – 3ins in k1, p1 rib, beg 2nd row p1. Change to 3¼mm (No 10) needles. Work 2 rows st-st, beg k.

Working in st-st, work 5 rows from chart A, reading k rows from right to left, rep chart 5 times excluding st beyond dotted line, then first 7 sts of chart again. For p rows read last 7 sts of chart from left to right then rep whole chart 5 times.

Work 2 rows LB, beg p and inc 2 sts evenly across 2nd row. 69 sts.

Now work 29 rows of chart B as for Back.

Work 2 rows LB, beg k and dec 2 sts evenly across 2nd row. 67 sts.

Now work from ** to ** as Back. This completes 74 rows of Fair Isle patt.

Front Shaping: Now rep 74 rows of Fair Isle patt, but dec 1 st at front edge at beg of next and every following 4th row until 13th row of chart B is completed.

Armhole Shaping: Shaping front edge as before, cast off 8 sts at beg of next row then dec 1 st at armhole edge on next 12 rows. Keeping armhole edge straight, dec at front edge as before on every 4th row until 30 sts remain. Cont straight until 2nd set of 74 rows is completed then rep 5 rows of chart A again. Cont in LB only. P 1 row, k 1 row. Cast off *loosely.*

Left Front

As Right Front, reversing front and armhole shapings.

Front Band

With 2¾mm (No 12) needles and LB cast on 10 sts. Work 4 rows in k1, p1 rib.

Buttonhole row: Rib 4, cast off 2, rib 4.
Next row: Rib 4, cast on 2, rib 4.

Cont in rib, making 4 more buttonholes 8cm – 3ins apart (measure from base of previous buttonhole with work slightly stretched). After 5th buttonhole cont in rib until band measures 135cm – 53ins from beg, slightly stretched. Cast off.

Armbands

Join shoulders. With 2¾mm (No 12) needles and LB pick up and k 140 sts evenly around armhole edge. Work 9 rows in k1, p1 rib. Cast off ribwise. Work 2nd armband to match.

Making up

Press lightly, omitting ribbing. Join side and armband seams. Sew on front band, placing buttonholes to right front for a woman and to left front for a man. Press seams. Sew on buttons.

Fair Isle Pullover

A traditional V-neck pullover in an all-over Fair Isle design. The pullover is made in light grey with eight contrast colours that are used in four bands of pattern repeated throughout.

The pattern is in two sizes, to fit from 86cm (34 inch) to 102cm (40 inch) bust or chest. The pullover is knitted in Shetland 2-ply Jumper Weight wool, which is a 4-ply equivalent. (See illustration page 88.)

Materials: Of Shetland Wool 2-ply Jumper Weight (4-ply equivalent): 2 (3) hanks (2-oz) Grey (shade 203), 1 (1) hank (2-oz) Off-White (1a), (1) 1 hank (1-oz) each Deep Pink (70), Green (47), Pale Blue (14), Deep Red (55), Royal Blue (18), Pale Pink (101) and Black (77); two each 3¼mm (No 10) and 2¾mm (No 12) needles.

Measurements: To fit 86–91 (96–102)cm – 34–36 (38–40)in bust or chest; length, 56 (61)cm – 22 (24)ins.

Tension: 14 sts and 15 rows to 5cm – 2ins over Fair Isle on 3¼mm (No 10) needles.

Abbreviations: See page 116.

Colour Abbreviation: G = Grey.

Back

With 2¾mm (No 12) needles and G cast on 127 (145) sts. Work 5cm – 2ins in k1, p1 rib, beg 2nd row p1. Change to 3¼mm (No 10) needles. Work 2 rows st-st, beg k. Still working in st-st work patt from chart, reading k rows from right to left and p rows from left to right and working 1 st beyond dotted line at end of k rows and beg of p rows only. Work in patt from chart until work measures 34 (37)cm – 13½ (14½)ins from beg, ending p.

Armhole Shaping: Cast off 10 sts at beg of next 2 rows then dec 1 st each end of next 8 rows. 91 (109) sts. Cont in patt until work measures 56 (61)cm – 22 (24)ins from beg, ending p.

Shoulder Shaping: Cast off 28 (34) sts loosely at beg of next 2 rows. Leave 34 (41) sts on spare needle.

Front

As Back until work measures 33 (36)cm – 13 (14)ins from beg, ending p.

Front Dividing row: Patt 61 (70), k2 tog, TURN. Work on these sts only for left side of front. Work 3 rows in patt.

Armhole Shaping: *Next row:* Cast off 10, patt to last 2 sts, k2 tog. Dec 1 st at armhole edge on next 8 rows, at same time dec at neck edge on 4th and 8th rows.* Keeping armhole edge straight, dec 1 st at neck edge on every 4th row until 28 (34) sts remain. Cont straight until work measures 56 (61)cm – 22 (24)ins from beg, ending p. Cast off loosely.

Return to remaining sts, place centre st on a safety pin, rejoin yarn and work: k2 tog, patt 61 (70) to end. Work 4 rows, dec 1 st at beg of 4th row.

Armhole Shaping: Cast off 10 sts at beg of next row. Dec 1 st at armhole edge on next 8 rows, at same time dec 1 st at neck edge on 3rd and 7th rows. Now complete to match left side of front from *.

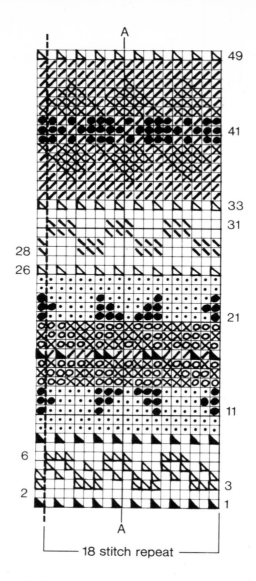

A

49

41

33

31

28
26

21

11

6

2

3

1

A

18 stitch repeat

This chart applies also to the Cardigan with Fair Isle Borders (page 83) and the Fair Isle Scarf, Hat and Gloves (page 87)

Neckband

Join right shoulder. With 2¾mm (No 12) needles and G pick up and k 67 (75) sts down left side of front neck, k st from safety pin, pick up and k 67 (75) sts up right side of front neck then k sts from back neck.

1st row: (K1, p1) to within 2 sts of centre-front st, p2 tog, p centre-front st, p2 tog tbl, p1, (k1, p1) to end.

2nd row: (K1, p1) to within 2 sts of centre-front st, skpo, k centre-front st, k2 tog, p1, (k1, p1) to end.

Rep last 2 rows 3 times more then 1st row again. (9 rows in all.) Cast off ribwise, dec each side of centre-front st while casting off.

Armbands

Join left shoulder and neckband seam. With 2¾mm (No 12) needles and G pick up and k136 (144) sts evenly around armhole edge. Work 9 rows in k1, p1 rib. Cast off ribwise. Work 2nd armband to match.

Making up

Press lightly, omitting ribbing. Join side and armband seams. Press seams.

Cardigan with Fair Isle Borders

A classic V-neck cardigan to pair with the preceding pullover. It is knitted in light grey with the same eight-colour Fair Isle pattern, repeated once around the back and fronts. The cardigan has raglan sleeves and the front band can be reversed as it is worked separately and sewn on afterwards.

Sizes and wool are the same as for the pullover. (See illustration page 88.)

Materials: Of Shetland Wool 2-ply Jumper Weight (4-ply equivalent): 6 (7) hanks (2-oz) Grey (shade 203), 1 (1) hank (2-oz) Off-White (1a), 1 (1) hank (1-oz) each Deep Pink (70), Green (47), Pale Blue (14), Deep Red (55), Royal Blue (18), Pale Pink (101) and Black (77); two each 3¼mm (No 10) and 2¾mm (No 12) needles; 5 buttons.

Measurements: To fit 86–91 (96–102)cm – 34–36 (38–40)in bust or chest; length, 61 (66)cm – 24 (26)ins; sleeve, 48 (51)cm – 19 (20)ins.

Tension: 14 sts and 18 rows to 5cm – 2ins over st-st on 3¼mm (No 10) needles.

Abbreviations: See page 116

Colour Abbreviation: G = Grey.

Back

With 2¾mm (No 12) needles and G cast on 127 (145) sts. Work 5cm – 2ins in k1, p1 rib, beg 2nd row p1. Change to 3¼mm (No 10) needles. Work 2 rows in st-st, beg k.

Now work 50 rows of chart (*see page 82*), reading k rows from right to left and p rows from left to right and working 1 st beyond dotted line at end of k rows and beg of p rows only.

Now cont in G only in st-st until work measures 38 (41)cm – 15 (16)ins from beg, ending p.

Raglan Shaping: *Cast off 3 (6) sts at beg of next 2 rows.
Next row: K2, skpo, k to last 4 sts, k2 tog, k2.
Next row: P.
Rep last 2 rows until 41 (45) sts remain, ending p. Cast off loosely.

Right Front

With 2¾mm (No 12) needles and G cast on 64 (73) sts. Work 5cm – 2ins in k1, p1 rib, beg 2nd row p1 for 2nd size only. Change to 3¼mm (No 10) needles. Work 2 rows st-st, beg k.

Now work from chart thus:
1st size: On k rows read chart from right to left and rep patt 3 times then rep first 10 sts of chart. On p rows read chart from left to right, beg at point 'A' on chart and work last 10 sts then rep patt 3 times completely from left to right.
2nd size: Read k rows from right to left and p rows from left to right and rep chart 4 times, working 1 st beyond dotted line at end of k rows and beg of p rows only.
Cont until 50 rows of chart are completed. Now cont in G only**.

Front Shaping: Working in st-st, beg k, dec 1 st at front edge at beg of next and every following 4th row until work measures 38 (41)cm – 15 (16)ins from beg, ending k.

Raglan Shaping: Cast off 3 (6) sts at beg of next row.

83

Next row: K to last 4 sts, k2 tog, k2.
Next row: P.
Still shaping front edge as before, rep last 2 rows for raglan shaping until 20 (22) decs have been worked in all at front edge. Keeping front edge straight, shape raglan as before until 3 (3) sts remain. Dec 1 st at front edge on next 2 alt rows. Fasten off.

Left Front

As Right Front to **.

Front Shaping: Working in st-st, beg k, dec 1 st at front edge at end of next and every following 4th row until work measures 38 (41)cm – 15 (16)ins from beg, ending p.

Raglan Shaping: Cast off 3 (6) sts at beg of next row.
Next row: P.
Next row: K2, skpo, k to end.
Rep these 2 rows for raglan shaping and complete to match Right Front.

Sleeves

With 2¾mm (No 12) needles and G cast on 55 (55) sts. Work 5cm – 2ins in k1, p1 rib, beg 2nd row p1.
Next row: Rib 1, (inc in next st, rib 2) to end. 73 (73) sts.

Change to 3¼mm (No 10) needles. Work 2 rows st-st, beg k. Now work 50 rows from chart as Back.

Cont in G only. Cont in st-st, inc 1 st each end of next and every following 8th (6th) row until there are 93 (107) sts. Cont straight until work measures 48 (51)cm – 19 (20)ins from beg, ending p.

Raglan Shaping: Work exactly as Back Raglan Shaping from * until 7 (7) sts remain, ending p. Cast off.

Front Band

With 2¾mm (No 12) needles and G cast on 12 (12) sts. Work 6 rows in k1, p1 rib.

Buttonhole row: Rib 5, cast off 3, rib 4.
Next row: Rib 4, cast on 3, rib 5.
Cont in rib, making 4 more buttonholes 5cm – 2ins apart with work slightly stretched. Cont in rib until band measures 142 (154)cm – 56 (60½)ins from beg, slightly stretched. Cast off.

Making up

Press lightly, omitting ribbing. Join raglan, side and sleeve seams. Sew on front band, placing buttonholes to right front for a woman and to left front for a man. Press seams. Sew on buttons.

Opposite: *Scarborough Guernsey with Monogram (page 23) and Fair Isle Button Up Jacket (page 94)*

Fair Isle Scarf, Hat and Gloves

A set using the same Fair Isle pattern as the preceding pullover and cardigan. The scarf is all in stocking stitch in double thickness for extra warmth and uses the full pattern repeat of the pullover and cardigan. The hat and gloves use only the first 33 and 27 rows respectively of the pattern repeat. The hat is ribbed under the brim for a close fit.

The hat and gloves are both in standard women's sizes. The wool is the same as that used for the pullover and cardigan. (See illustration overleaf.)

Materials: *For set:* Of Shetland Wool 2-ply Jumper Weight (4-ply equivalent): 4 hanks (2-oz) Grey (shade 203), 1 hank (2-oz) Off-White (1a), 1 hank (1-oz) each Deep Pink (70), Green (47), Pale Blue (14), Deep Red (55), Royal Blue (18), Pale Pink (101) and Black (77); *for Scarf alone:* 2 hanks Grey and 1 hank each of 8 contrast shades; *for Hat or Gloves alone:* 1 hank Grey and 1 hank each of 8 contrast shades; two each $3\frac{1}{4}$mm (No 10) and $2\frac{3}{4}$mm (No 12) needles.

Sizes: *Scarf:* Length, 152cm – 60ins; *Hat and Gloves:* To fit average woman's head and hand.

Tension: 14 sts and 15 rows to 5cm – 2ins over Fair Isle on $3\frac{1}{4}$mm (No 10) needles.

Abbreviations: See page 116.

Colour Abbreviations: G = Grey.

Opposite: Fair Isle Pullover (page 81) and Cardigan (page 83)

SCARF

To Make: With $3\frac{1}{4}$mm (No 10) needles and G cast on 109 sts. Work 6 rows g-st (every row k). Work 10 rows st-st, beg k.
Now work 49 rows of chart (*see page 82*), reading k rows from right to left and p rows from left to right and working 1 st beyond dotted line at end of k rows and beg of p rows only.
Now work 36cm – 14ins in st-st in G only, ending p.
Turn chart upside down and work row 49 back to row 1, then turn chart right way up and work row 2 to row 49.
Work 36cm – 14ins in st-st in G only, ending p. Turn chart upside down and work row 49 back to row 1. With G only work 10 rows st-st, beg p, and then 6 rows g-st. Cast off loosely.
Press scarf lightly. Fold in half lengthways, right sides tog, and join one end and one side seam. Turn out to right side and join other end. Press.

HAT

To Make: With $2\frac{3}{4}$mm (No 12) needles and G cast on 145 sts. Work 4 rows in k1, p1 rib, beg 2nd row p1. Change to $3\frac{1}{4}$mm (No 10) needles. Work 2 rows st-st, beg k.
Now work rows 1 to 33 of chart (*see page 82*), reading rows as for Scarf.

Fair Isle Scarf, Hat and Gloves

Cont in G only. Work 4 rows st-st, beg p, dec 1 st at end of last row. 144 sts. Change to 2¾mm (No 12) needles and work 14cm – 5½ins in k1, p1 rib, ending with a right side row.

Top Shaping: *Next row:* (right side for crown). (K10, k2 tog) 12 times. P 1 row.

K 7 k2tog 10 times

Next row: (K9, k2 tog) 12 times. P 1 row.
Next row: (K8, k2 tog) 12 times.
Dec in this way on every k row until 24 sts remain.
Next row: (P2 tog) 12 times.
Break yarn leaving long end for sewing, thread through 12 sts, draw up and secure then join back seam. Press st-st parts only. Turn back Fair Isle brim.

88

GLOVES

Right Hand

With 2¾mm (No 12) needles and G cast on 50 sts. Work 6cm – 2½ins in k1, p1 rib.

Next row: (Inc in next st, rib 9) to end. 55 sts. Change to 3¼mm (No 10) needles. Work 4 rows st-st, beg k*.

Now work rows 1 to 9 of chart (*see page 82*), reading rows as for Scarf.

Thumb Shaping: With Pale Blue p28, cast on 9, TURN. Cont in G only. K18, TURN. Work 5½cm – 2¼ins in st-st on these 18 sts for thumb, ending p.

Next row: (K2 tog) 9 times.

Break yarn leaving end for sewing, thread through 9 sts, draw up and secure then join thumb seam.

With wrong side facing rejoin Pale Blue and p27 to end.

Next row: Working from 11th row of chart, k27, with Pale Blue pick up and k 9 sts from base of thumb, k19 to end. 55 sts.

Cont from chart until 27th row of chart is completed. Cont in G only.

**1st Finger: P35, TURN, k15, TURN. Work 6½cm – 2½ins in st-st on these 15 sts, ending p.

Next row: K1, (k2 tog) 7 times.

Break yarn leaving end for sewing, thread through 8 sts, draw up and secure then join finger seam.

2nd Finger: With wrong side facing pick up and k 2 sts from base of 1st finger purlwise, p7, TURN, k16, TURN. Work 8cm – 3ins in st-st on these 16 sts, ending p.

Next row: (K2 tog) 8 times.

Break yarn leaving end for sewing, thread through 8 sts, draw up and secure then join finger seam.

3rd Finger: Work exactly as 2nd finger but pick up 2 sts from base of 2nd finger.

4th Finger: With wrong side facing pick up and k 2 sts from base of 3rd finger purlwise, p6 to end, TURN, k14. Work 5cm – 2ins in st-st on these 14 sts, ending p.

Next row: (K2 tog) 7 times.

Break yarn leaving long end for sewing, thread through 7 sts, draw up and secure then join side seam of glove. Press lightly, omitting ribbing.

Left Hand

As Right Hand to *.
Now work rows 1 to 8 of chart.

Thumb Shaping: With Pale Blue k28, cast on 9, TURN, p18, TURN. Cont in G only and complete thumb as Right Hand.

With right side facing rejoin Pale Blue and k27 to end.

Next row: With Pale Blue p27, pick up and p 9 sts from base of thumb, p19 to end. 55 sts.

Cont from chart until 27th row of chart is completed. Cont in G only and complete as Right Hand from **.

89

Fair Isle Zipped Jacket

An intricate design using seven colours on a natural background in a varying combination of wide and narrow, complicated and simple bands of Fair Isle pattern. These bands change all the way up the back and fronts and are different again on the sleeves. Soft shades of brown are combined with green, navy, white, heather and pink. The ribbed front bands and collar are worked afterwards.

The pattern is in two sizes, to fit from 86cm (34 inch) to 102cm (40 inch) bust or chest. The jacket is knitted in Scottish Homespun wool, which is a double knitting equivalent. (See illustration page 103.)

Materials: Of Scottish Homespun Wool (Double Knitting equivalent): 3 (4) hanks (2-oz) Natural, 1 (1) hank each Dark Brown, Green, White, Navy, Mid Brown, Pink and Heather; two each 3¼mm (No 10) and 4mm (No 8) needles; 46 (51)cm – 18 (20)in open-ended cardigan zip.

Measurements: To fit 86–91 (97–102)cm – 34–36 (38–40)in bust or chest; length, 56 (61)cm – 22 (24)ins; sleeve, 48 (51)cm – 19 (20)ins.

Tension: 11 sts and 12 rows to 5cm – 2ins over Fair Isle on 4mm (No 8) needles.

Abbreviations: See page 116.

Colour Abbreviation: N = Natural.

Back

With 3¼mm (No 10) needles and N cast on 108 (120) sts. Work 8 (10)cm – 3 (4)ins in k1, p1 rib. Change to 4mm (No 8) needles. Work 2 (8) rows in st-st, beg k. Still working in st-st, work first 38 rows of chart A, rep 12-st patt 9 (10) times in each row and reading k rows from right to left and p rows from left to right and dec 3 sts evenly across 38th row *for 1st size only*. 105 (120) sts.

Now work 39th to 53rd rows of chart thus: *For 1st size: For k rows rep chart 3 times then first 15 sts of chart to point 'A'. For p rows beg at point 'A' and work last 15 sts of chart then rep whole chart 3 times.*
For 2nd size: Rep chart 4 times in each row.

Work 54th row of chart dec 1 st at end of row *for 1st size only*. 104 (120) sts.
Work 55th to 62nd rows of chart.
Work 63rd row, inc 1 st at end of row *for 1st size* and dec 1 st at end of row *for 2nd size*. 105 (119) sts.

Now work 64th to 76th rows of chart thus: *Both sizes: For k rows rep chart 7 (8) times then first 7 sts of chart to point 'B'. For p rows beg at point 'B' and work last 7 sts of chart then rep whole chart 7 (8) times.*

Work 77th row, dec 1 st at end of row *for 1st size* and inc 1 st at end of row *for 2nd size*. 104 (120) sts.
Work 78th to 85th rows of chart.
Work 86th row, inc 1 st at end of row *for 1st size only*. 105 (120) sts.

Now work 87th to 103rd rows of chart as for rows 39 to 53, but reading point 'C' for point 'A' for 1st size.

Work 104th row, dec 1 st at end of row *for 1st size only*. 104 (120) sts.
Now work 105th to 114th rows of chart. Work 2 rows all in Navy.

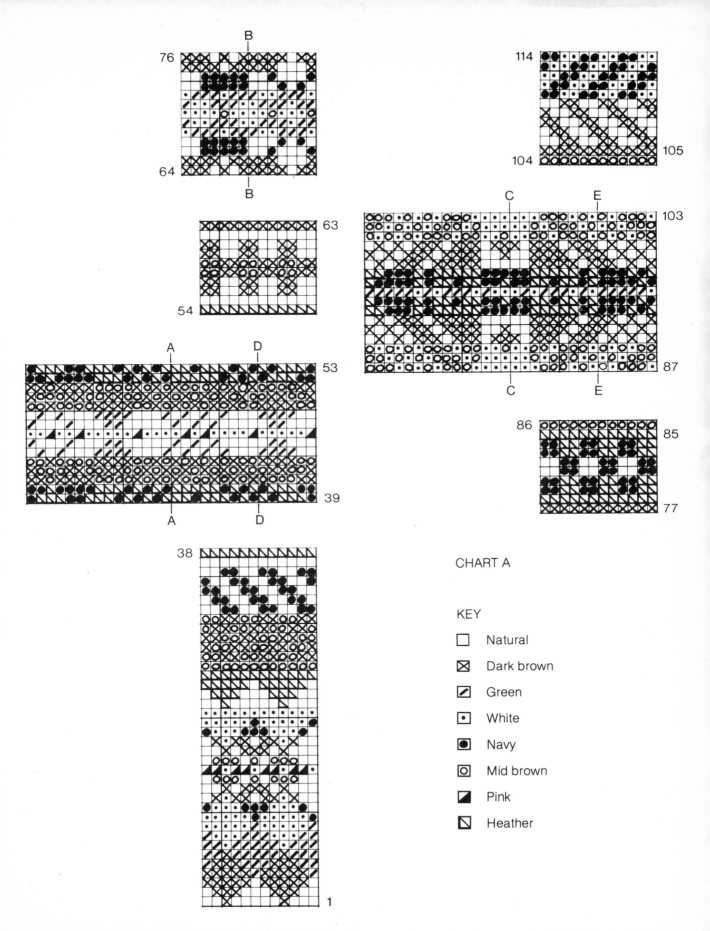

CHART A

KEY

- ☐ Natural
- ☒ Dark brown
- ☑ Green
- ⊡ White
- ⬤ Navy
- ◉ Mid brown
- ◤ Pink
- ◥ Heather

Shoulder Shaping: With Navy cast off 34 (40) sts loosely at beg of next 2 rows. Leave 36 (40) sts on spare needle.

Right Front

With $3\frac{1}{4}$mm (No 10) needles and N cast on 54 (60) sts. Work 8 (10)cm – 3 (4)ins in k1, p1 rib. Change to 4mm (No 8) needles. Work 2 (8) rows in st-st, beg k.

Now work first 38 rows of chart A thus:
For 1st size: For k rows rep chart 4 times then first 6 sts of chart. *For p rows* beg at centre of chart and work last 6 sts then rep whole chart 4 times.
For 2nd size: Rep chart 5 times in each row.

Work 39th to 53rd rows of chart thus:
For 1st size: For k rows beg at point 'D' and work last 24 sts of chart then work whole chart once. *For p rows* work whole chart then first 24 sts to point 'D'.
For 2nd size: Rep chart twice in each row.

Work 54th row of chart, inc 1 st each end of row *for 1st size only.* 56 (60) sts.

Work 55th to 63rd rows of chart.

Work 64th to 76th rows of chart thus:
For 1st size: Rep chart 4 times in each row.
For 2nd size: For k rows rep chart 4 times then first 4 sts again. *For p rows* work last 4 sts of chart then rep whole chart 4 times.

Work 77th to 85th rows of chart.

Work 86th row, dec 1 st each end of row *for 1st size only.* 54 (60) sts.

Now work 87th to 103rd rows of chart as for rows 39 to 53, but reading point 'E' for point 'D' *for 1st size.*

Work 104th row.

Neck Shaping: With Dark Brown cast off 14 sts at beg of next row. Now work from row 106 of chart and dec 1 st at neck edge on next 6 rows. 34 (40) sts. Work last 5 rows of chart then 2 rows in Navy. Cast off *loosely* in Navy.

Left Front

Work exactly as for Right Front *but beg st-st with a p row* instead of a k row, thus reversing Fair Isle patt and neck shaping.

Sleeves

With $3\frac{1}{4}$mm (No 10) needles and N cast on 51 (60) sts. Work 8 (10)cm – 3 (4)ins in k1, p1 rib, beg 2nd row p1 *for 1st size only.*
Next row: Rib 6 (6), *inc in next st, rib 4 (2); rep from * to end. 60 (78) sts.

Change to 4mm (No 8) needles. Work 2 rows in st-st, beg k.

Now work first 35 rows of chart B, inc 1 st each end of 5th and every following 6th row until there are 72 (90) sts.

Now work 36th to 41st rows of chart, inc 6 sts evenly across 41st row *for 2nd size only.* 72 (96) sts.

Work 42nd to 60th rows of chart, rep patt 3 (4) times in each row.

Now work 61st to 95th rows of chart, inc 1 st each end of next and every following 6th row until there are 84 (100) sts. Work 1 row more in Heather after 95th row. Cast off *loosely.*

Front Bands and Collar

Join shoulders. With $3\frac{1}{4}$mm (No 10) needles and N cast on 10 (10) sts. Work in k1, p1 rib until band reaches up left front to beg of neck shaping, slightly stretched**. Leave sts on spare needle. Work right front band to match to **.
Next row: Rib 10, pick up and k 27 (28) sts around right side of front neck, work across back-neck sts thus: (inc in next st, rib 3) 9 (10) times, pick up and k 28 (28) sts around left side of front neck then rib 10 sts from spare needle. 120 (126) sts. Work 12cm – $4\frac{3}{4}$ins in k1, p1 rib. Cast off loosely ribwise.

Making up

Press lightly, omitting rib. Sew cast-off edges of sleeves to sides of back and fronts, beg and ending 19 (23)cm – $7\frac{1}{2}$ (9)ins from shoulder seams. Join side and sleeve seams. Sew in zip. Press seams.

60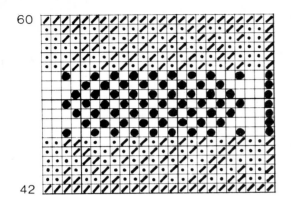
42

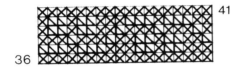
41
36
35

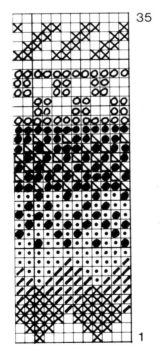
1

95
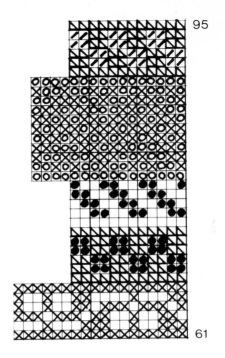
61

CHART B

KEY

☐ Natural

☒ Dark brown

◪ Green

⊡ White

⊙ Navy

◧ Heather

⊚ Mid brown

Fair Isle Button Up Jacket

A long jacket worked in broad, alternating bands of traditional Fair Isle pattern. The colours used in the example shown (bottle green, Ming green and white) are not traditional, but the jacket could equally well be made in classic Fair Isle shades, using a pale, natural background and two darker colours for the pattern. The jacket has hemmed lower and sleeve edges and ribbed neckband and front bands.

The pattern is in two sizes, to fit from 86cm (34 inch) to 102cm (40 inch) bust. The jacket is knitted in double knitting wool. (See illustration page 85.)

Materials: Of Lister-Lee Motoravia Double Knitting: 17 (19) balls (25-gr) Bottle (shade 1812), 4 (5) balls Ming Green (401) and Arctic White (102); two each 4mm (No 8) and 3¼mm (No 10) needles; 10 buttons.

Measurements: To fit 86–91 (96–102)cm – 34–36 (38–40)in bust; length, 63cm – 25ins; sleeve, 48cm – 19ins.

Tension: 11 sts and 13 rows to 5cm – 2ins over Fair Isle on 4mm (No 8) needles.

Abbreviations: See page 116.

Colour Abbreviation: B = Bottle.

Back

With 3¼mm (No 10) needles and B cast on 101 (109) sts. Work 6 rows st-st, beg p. Now k 1 row for hemline. Change to 4mm (No 8) needles. Work 8 rows st-st, beg k.

Now working in st-st, work from chart patt thus*:

1st size: For k rows beg at point 'A' and work last 32 sts of chart, reading from right to left, then work all 36 sts of chart then work first 33 sts of chart to point 'B'. For p rows beg at point 'B' and work last 33 sts of chart, reading from left to right, then work all 36 sts of chart then work first 32 sts of chart to point 'A'.

2nd size: Reading k rows from right to left and p rows from left to right, rep chart 3 times then first st of chart again at end of k rows and beg of p rows. Cont from chart until 71st row of 2nd complete chart rep has been worked.

Now cont in B only. Work 9 rows st-st, beg p.

Shoulder Shaping: Cast off 32 (35) sts *loosely* at beg of next 2 rows. Leave 37 (39) sts on spare needle.

Right Front

With 3¼mm (No 10) needles and B cast on 52 (57) sts. Work as Back to *.

1st size: For k rows beg at point 'C' and work last 19 sts of chart then work first 33 sts of chart to point 'B'. For p rows beg at point 'B' and work last 33 sts of chart then work first 19 sts of chart to point 'C'.

2nd size: For k rows beg at point 'D' and work last 21 sts of chart then rep all 36 sts of chart. *For p rows* rep all 36 sts of chart then first 21 sts to point 'D'.

Cont from chart until 71st row of 2nd complete chart rep has been worked.

Now cont in B only. P 1 row.

Neck Shaping: Cast off 14 (16) sts at beg of next row then dec 1 st at neck edge on next 6 rows. 32 (35) sts. Work 2 rows straight. Cast off *loosely*.

KEY

☐ Bottle

☒ Ming

⊡ White

36 stitch repeat

Left Front

As Right Front, BUT work p for k and k for p *throughout*, thus reversing pattern and neck shaping.

Sleeves

With $3\frac{1}{4}$mm (No 10) needles and B cast on 73 (73) sts. Work as Back to *.

For both sizes: Start at row 41 of chart and reading k rows from right to left and p rows from left to right, rep chart twice then first st of chart again at end of k rows and beg of p rows. Cont until first patt band has been worked (to row 71) then cont to end of chart then rep whole 78 rows of chart, *at same time* inc 1 st each end of next and every following 8th row until there are 87 (87) sts, working extra sts into chart patt. When 78th row of chart rep is completed, cast off *loosely*.

Neckband

Join shoulders. With $3\frac{1}{4}$mm (No 10) needles and B pick up and k 22 (24) sts around right side of front neck, k sts from back neck then pick up and k 22 (24) sts around left side of front neck. 81 (87) sts. Work 8cm – 3ins in k1, p1 rib,

beg 2nd row p1. Cast off loosely ribwise. Fold neckband in half to wrong side and sew down lightly.

Front Bands

With $3\frac{1}{4}$mm (No 10) needles and B cast on 10 sts. Work in k1, p1 rib until band reaches from front hemline to top of doubled neckband, slightly stretched. Cast off. With $3\frac{1}{4}$mm (No 10) needles and B cast on 10 sts. Work 4 rows in k1, p1 rib.

Buttonhole row: Rib 4, cast off 2, rib 4.
Next row: Rib 4, cast on 2, rib 4.

Cont in rib, making 9 more buttonholes 7cm – $2\frac{3}{4}$ins apart (measure from base of previous buttonhole with work slightly stretched). After 10th buttonhole is completed, cont in rib until band is same length as first band. Cast off.

Making up

Press lightly, omitting rib. Sew cast-off edges of sleeves to sides of back and fronts, beg and ending 20cm – 8ins from shoulder seams. Join side and sleeve seams. Fold in and sew down hems at lower and sleeve edges. Sew on front bands, placing cast-on edges to top of neckband. Press seams. Sew on buttons.

Baby's Cardigan with Fair Isle Borders

A baby's cardigan in off-white with a four-colour Fair Isle border around the lower edge. Five rows in one colour are repeated at the sleeve edges. The jacket has raglan sleeves, garter stitch main borders and ribbed cuffs.

The pattern is in one size only, to fit 46–51cm (18–20 inch) chest. The cardigan is knitted in Shetland 2-ply Lace Weight wool, which is a 4-ply equivalent.

Baby's Cardigan with Fair Isle Borders

Materials: Of Shetland 2-ply Lace Weight Wool: 3 hanks (1-oz) Off-White (shade L1A), 1 hank each Navy (L36), Blue (L16), Purple (L44) and Pink (L70); two $2\frac{3}{4}$mm (No 12) needles; 3 buttons.

Measurements: To fit 46–51cm – 18–20in chest; length, 25cm – 10ins; sleeve, 14cm – $5\frac{1}{2}$ins.

Tension: 16 sts and 24 rows to 5cm – 2ins over stocking stitch on $2\frac{3}{4}$mm (No 12) needles.

Abbreviations: See page 116.

Colour Abbreviation: W = White.

Main Part

With $2\frac{3}{4}$mm (No 12) needles and W cast on 183 sts. Work 8 rows in g-st (every row k).
Next row: K.
Next row: K8, p to last 8 sts, k8.
These 2 rows form st-st with 8-st g-st front borders.

Working in st-st with g-st borders, work 31 rows from chart on st-st thus:
For k rows read chart from right to left and work 4-st rep for first and last 5 rows, plus 3 sts at end, then for centre 15 rows work: 8 sts before point 'A' then rep 30 st from point 'A' to point 'B' 5 times then 9 sts beyond point 'B' once.

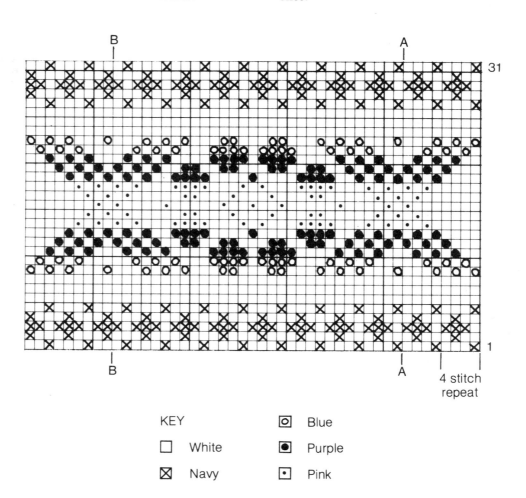

KEY

☐ White

☒ Navy

◙ Blue

◉ Purple

⊡ Pink

For p rows read chart from left to right and work 3 end sts then 4-st rep for first and last 5 rows, then for centre 15 rows work 9 sts before point 'B' then rep from point 'B' to point 'A' 5 times then 8 sts beyond point 'A'.

When chart is completed cont in W only until work measures 14cm – 5½ins from beg, ending p.

Armhole Dividing row: K46, cast off 4 for right armhole, k83, cast off 4 for left armhole, k46. Work on last set of sts for **Left Front.**

Raglan Shaping: *Next row:* K8, p to end.
Next row: K2, skpo, k to end.
Rep last 2 rows until 24 sts remain.

Neck Shaping: *Next row:* (wrong side). K8 and place these 8 sts on a safety pin, p to end. Shaping raglan as before, dec 1 st at neck edge on next 8 rows. 4 sts. Dec 1 st at neck edge only on next 3 rows. Fasten off.

Rejoin W to wrong side of centre set of sts for **Back.**

Raglan Shaping: *Next row:* P.
Next row: K2, skpo, k to last 4 sts, k2 tog, k2.
Rep last 2 rows until 29 sts remain. P 1 row.
Leave sts on spare needle.

Rejoin W to wrong side of remaining sts for **Right Front.**

Raglan Shaping: *Next row:* P to last 8 sts, k8.
Next row: K4, yarn forward to make a loop st, k2 tog, k to last 4 sts, k2 tog, k2.
Shape raglan in this way, making 2nd buttonhole when 34 sts remain, until 24 sts remain. Work 1 row.

Neck Shaping: *Next row:* K8 and place these 8 sts on a safety pin, k2 tog, k10, k2 tog, k2.

Shaping raglan as before, dec 1 st at neck edge on next 7 rows. 4 sts. Dec 1 st at neck edge only on next 3 rows. Fasten off.

Sleeves

With 2¾mm (No 12) needles and W cast on 48 sts. Work 12 rows in k1, p1 rib. Work 2 rows st-st, beg k. Now work first 5 rows of chart, working 4-st rep 12 times in each row.

Cont in W only, inc 1 st each end of every 4th row until there are 64 sts. Cont straight until work measures 14cm – 5½ins from beg, ending p.

Raglan Shaping: Cast off 2 sts at beg of next 2 rows.
Next row: K2, skpo, k to last 4 sts, k2 tog, k2.
Next row: P.
Rep last 2 rows until 6 sts remain, ending p. Leave sts on spare needle.

Neckband

Join all raglan seams. Place 8 sts at right front edge on to a 2¾mm (No 12) needle then with W pick up and k 12 sts around right side of front neck, k sts from right sleeve, back and left sleeve, pick up and k 12 sts around left side of front neck then k 8 sts at left front edge. 81 sts. Work 7 rows in g-st, making 3rd buttonhole at beg of 4th row as before. Cast off.

Making up

Press lightly, omitting ribbing. Join sleeve seams. Sew on buttons.

Shetland Sweater

A striking all-over Shetland design in just two colours – blue and off-white. In a strictly traditional garment, a neutral brown or grey would be used instead of blue.

The pattern is in two sizes, to fit 86–91cm (34–36 inch) or 102–107cm (40–42 inch) bust or chest. The gap between sizes is due to the wide pattern repeat. Double knitting wool is used in the example shown. For a more traditional texture, Scottish Homespun or Shetland 3-ply, both double knitting equivalents, could be used. (See illustration page 52.)

Materials: Of Double Knitting Wool: 7 (9) balls (50-gr) Main Colour (Blue), 5 (7) balls (50-gr) Contrast (Off-White); two each 4mm (No 8) and $3\frac{1}{4}$mm (No 10) needles.

Measurements: To fit 86–91 (102–107)cm – 34–36 (40–42)in bust or chest; length, 63 (68)cm – 25 (27)ins; sleeve, 56 (61)cm – 22 (24)ins.

Tension: 11 sts and 12 rows to 5cm – 2ins over Fair Isle on 4mm (No 8) needles.

Abbreviations: See page 116.

Colour Abbreviations: M = Main Colour; C = Contrast.

Back

With $3\frac{1}{4}$mm (No 10) needles and M cast on 96 (120) sts. Work 16 rows in k2, p2 rib, inc 1 st at end of last row. 97 (121) sts.

Change to 4mm (No 8) needles and work 2 rows st-st, beg k. Still working in st-st join C and work patt from chart, reading k rows from right to left and p rows from left to right and working 1 st beyond dotted line at end of k rows and beg of p rows only. When 34 rows are completed rep from 11th to 34th rows for 24-row main patt throughout until work measures 63 (68)cm – 25 (27)ins from beg, ending p.

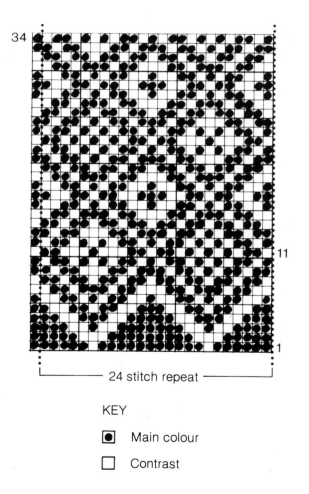

34

11

1

└──── 24 stitch repeat ────┘

KEY

◉ Main colour

☐ Contrast

Shoulder Shaping: Cast off 30 (40) sts *loosely* at beg of next 2 rows. Leave 37 (41) sts on spare needle.

Front

As Back until work measures 59 (64)cm – 23½ (25½)ins from beg, ending p.

Neck Shaping: *Next row:* Patt 34 (44), k2 tog, TURN. Work on these sts only.
Dec 1 st at neck edge on next 5 rows. 30 (40) sts. Work 4 rows straight. Cast off *loosely*. Place centre 25 (29) sts on a st holder. Complete other side of neck to match.

Sleeves

With 3¼mm (No 10) needles and M cast on 48 (48) sts. Work 16 rows in k2, p2 rib, inc 1 st at end of last row. 49 (49) sts.

Change to 4mm (No 8) needles and work 2 rows in st-st, beg k. Now join C and work from chart to match Back, but inc 1 st each end of every 4th row until there are 97 (109) sts, working extra sts into Fair Isle patt. Cont straight until work measures 56 (61)cm – 22 (24)ins from beg. Cast off *loosely*.

Neckband

Join right shoulder. With 3¼mm (No 10) needles and M pick up and k 11 sts down left side of front neck, k sts from st holder, pick up and k 11 sts up right side of front neck then k sts from back neck. 84 (92) sts. Work 7 rows in k2, p2 rib. Cast off *loosely ribwise*.

Making up

Press lightly, omitting ribbing. Join left shoulder and neckband seam. Sew cast-off edges of sleeves to sides of back and front, beg and ending 23 (25)cm – 9 (10)ins from shoulder seams. Join side and sleeve seams. Press seams lightly.

Shetland Pullover

A traditional geometric Shetland design with no less than five variations on the basic diamond pattern with crosses in between. The pullover is worked in the soft Shetland shades of natural, mid brown, dark brown and off-white, with just a touch of green.

The pattern is in two sizes, to fit 81–86cm (32–34 inch) or 97–102cm (38–40 inch) bust or chest. The gap between sizes is due to the wide pattern repeat. The pullover is knitted in Scottish Homespun wool, which is a double knitting equivalent. (See illustration page 103.)

Materials: Of Scottish Homespun Wool (Double Knitting equivalent): 3 (4) hanks (2-oz) Natural, 2 (2) hanks each Dark Brown and Mid Brown, 1 (1) hank each Off-White and Green; two each 4mm (No 8) and 3¼mm (No 10) needles.

Measurements: To fit 81–86 (97–102)cm – 32–34 (38–40)in bust or chest; length, 58 (62)cm – 23 (24½)ins.

Tension: 11 sts and 12 rows to 5cm – 2ins over Fair Isle on 4mm (No 8) needles.

Abbreviations: See page 116.

Colour Abbreviations: N = Natural; DB = Dark Brown; MB = Mid Brown.

Back

With 3¼mm (No 10) needles and DB cast on 91 (109) sts. Work 3 rows in k1, p1 rib, beg 2nd row p1. Break off DB and join MB. Rib 2 rows. Break off MB and join N. Rib 13 rows. Change to 4mm (No 8) needles and work 2 rows in st-st, beg k. Now begin chart (see page 105).

Still working in st-st, work from chart thus: *1st size: For k rows* read chart from right to left and rep chart 3 times excluding st beyond dotted line then work first 19 sts of chart to point 'A'. *For p rows* read chart from left to right and beg at point 'A' and work last 19 sts of chart then rep whole chart patt 3 times from dotted line.

2nd size: Reading k rows from right to left and p rows from left to right, rep chart 4 times, working 1 st beyond dotted line at end of k rows and beg of p rows only.

Work from chart until work measures 37 (39)cm – 14½ (15½)ins from beg.

Armhole Shaping: Keeping chart patt in line, cast off 6 sts at beg of next 2 rows then dec 1 st each end of next 3 (6) rows. 73 (85) sts. Cont in patt until work measures 58 (62)cm – 23 (24½)ins from beg, ending p.

Shoulder Shaping: Cast off 19 (23) sts loosely at beg of next 2 rows. Leave 35 (39) sts on spare needle.

Front

As Back until work measures 34 (37)cm – 13½ (14½)ins from beg, ending p.

Opposite: Shetland Pullover (above) and Fair Isle Zipped Jacket (page 90)

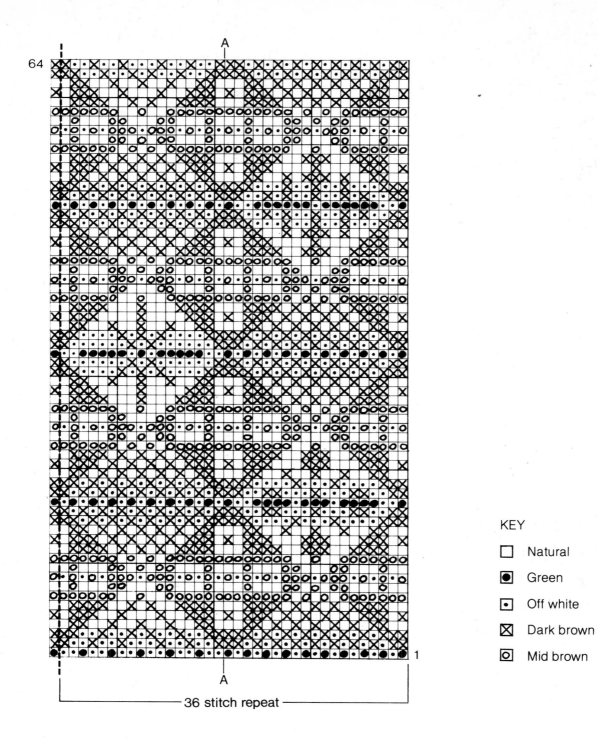

64

A

KEY

☐ Natural

◉ Green

⊡ Off white

☒ Dark brown

◻️ Mid brown

1

A

— 36 stitch repeat —

Opposite: *Aran Cardigan (page 66) and Fair Isle Waistcoat (page 78)*

Front Dividing row: Patt 43 (52), k2 tog, TURN. Work on these sts only. Work 5 rows, dec 1 st at front edge at beg of 3rd row.

Armhole Shaping: Dec at front edge on next and every following 3rd row, cast off 6 sts at beg of next row then dec 1 st at armhole edge on next 3 (6) rows.

*Keeping armhole edge straight, dec at front edge as before until 19 (23) sts remain. Cont straight until work is same length as Back to shoulder. Cast off *loosely*. Place centre st on a safety pin, rejoin yarn and patt across remaining 45 (54) sts thus: k2 tog, patt to end. Work 6 rows, dec 1 st at front edge at end of 3rd and beg of 6th row.

Armhole Shaping: Dec at front edge on every 3rd row, cast off 6 sts at beg of next row then dec 1 st at armhole edge on next 3 (6) rows. Now complete as left side of front from *.

Neckband

Join right shoulder. With 3¼mm (No 10) needles and N pick up and k 50 (56) sts down left side of front neck, k st from safety pin, pick up and k50 (56) sts up right side of front neck then k sts from back neck.

1st row: K1, (p1, k1) to within 2 sts of centre-front st, p2 tog, p centre-front st, p2 tog tbl, (k1, p1) to end.

2nd row: K1, (p1, k1) to within 2 sts of centre-front st, skpo, k centre-front st, k2 tog, (k1, p1) to end.

Rep last 2 rows 3 times more. Cast off ribwise, dec each side of centre-front st while casting off.

Armbands

Join left shoulder and neckband seam. With 3¼mm (No 10) needles and N pick up and k 116 (124) sts evenly around one armhole edge. Work 8 rows in k1, p1 rib. Cast off ribwise. Work 2nd armband to match.

Making up

Press lightly, omitting rib. Join side and armband seams. Press seams.

Shetland Cardigan

An all-over Shetland design for a woman or girl, using alternating bands of dark pattern on a light background and light pattern on a dark background. Although colours used in Shetland knitting are generally subdued, traditionally one strong colour may be introduced into a pattern. In the example shown, red is used to contrast with muted browns and off-white. The front band is worked separately and sewn on afterwards.

The pattern is in three sizes, to fit from 74cm (29 inch) to 94cm (37 inch) chest or bust. The cardigan is knitted in Shetland 2-ply Jumper Weight wool, which is a 4-ply equivalent. (See illustration page 33.)

Materials: Of Shetland Wool 2-ply Jumper Weight (4-ply equivalent): 6 (6:7) hanks (2-oz) Dark Brown (shade 5), 1 (2:2) hanks (2-oz) Off-White (1a), 1 (1:1) hank (2-oz) each Light Brown (3) and Mid Brown (4), 1 (1:1) hank (1-oz) Red (93); two each 3¾mm (No 9) and 3mm (No 11) needles; 5 buttons.

Measurements: To fit 74–79 (81–86:89–94)cm – 29–31 (32–34:35–37)in chest or bust; length, 51 (53:56)cm – 20 (21:22)ins; sleeve, 53 (56:58)cm – 21 (22:23)ins.

Tension: 14 sts and 15 rows to 5cm – 2ins over Fair Isle on 3¾mm (No 9) needles.

Abbreviations: See page 116.

Colour Abbreviation: DB = Dark Brown.

Back

With 3mm (No 11) needles and DB cast on 88 (98:108) sts. Work 9cm – 3½ins in k2, p2 rib, beg 2nd row p2 *for 2nd size only*. Change to 3¾mm (No 9) needles.
Next row: Rib 4 (6:8), (inc in next st, rib 3) to end. 109 (121:133) sts. Work 2 (8:12) rows in st-st, beg k.

Still working in st-st, work from chart thus:
1st and 3rd sizes: For k rows read chart from right to left and beg at point 'A' and work last 12 sts of chart to dotted line then rep all 24 sts of chart, working st beyond dotted line at end of row only. *For p rows* read chart from left to right and work st beyond dotted line then rep all 24 sts of chart, ending row at point 'A'.
For 2nd size: Read k rows from right to left and p rows from left to right and work st beyond dotted line at end of k rows and beg of p rows only.

Work 46 rows of chart twice then first 32 rows again. Now cont in DB only. Work 2 (4:6) rows st-st.

Shoulder Shaping: Cast off 35 (40:45) sts loosely at beg of next 2 rows. Cast off remaining 39 (41:43) sts.

Right Front

With 3mm (No 11) needles and DB cast on 50 (50:60) sts. Work 9cm – 3½ins in k2, p2 rib, beg 2nd row p2 *for 1st and 2nd sizes only*. Change to 3¾mm (No 9) needles.
Next row: Rib 6 (6:8), (inc in next st, rib 3) to end. 61 (61:73) sts.

Work 2 (8:12) rows in st-st, beg k.

Now work from chart thus:

1st and 2nd sizes: For *k rows* rep whole chart twice, omitting st beyond dotted line then work first 13 sts of chart again. For *p rows* beg 1 st to left of point 'A' and work last 13 sts of chart then rep whole chart twice from dotted line.

3rd size: Work whole chart 3 times in each row, working st beyond dotted line at end of k rows and beg of p rows only.

Work 46 rows of chart then work first 20 rows again.

Front Shaping: Cont from chart and dec 1 st at front edge at beg of next and every following alternate row until 35 (40:45) sts remain. Cont straight until 2 complete chart patts and 32 rows are completed. With DB only work 2 (4:6) rows more. Cast off loosely.

Left Front

As Right Front, reversing front shaping.

Sleeves

With 3mm (No 11) needles and DB cast on 56 (56:56) sts. Work 11cm – 4½in in k2, p2 rib. Change to 3¾mm (No 9) needles.

Next row: Rib 5, (inc in next st, rib 2) to end. 73 (73:73) sts.

Work 2 (8:12) rows in st-st, beg k.

Now work from chart, rep patt 3 times and working st beyond dotted line at end of k and beg of p rows only, *at same time* inc 1 st each end of every 6th row until there are 111 (111: 111) sts, working extra sts into chart patt. Cont straight until 2 complete chart patts plus 32 rows have been completed. With DB work 2 (4:6) rows more. Cast off *loosely.*

Front Band

Join shoulders. With 3mm (No 11) needles and DB cast on 10 sts. Work 6 rows in k2, p2 rib, beg 2nd row p2.

Buttonhole row: Rib 4, cast off 2, rib 4.

Next row: Rib 4, cast on 2, rib 4.

Cont in rib, making 4 more buttonholes 6 (6: 6½)cm – 2¼ (2¼:2½)ins apart (measure from *base* of previous buttonhole with work slightly stretched). Cont in rib after 5th buttonhole until band reaches up front, across back neck and down 2nd front, slightly stretched. Cast off.

Making up

Press lightly, omitting rib. Sew cast-off edges of sleeves to sides of back and fronts, beg and ending 20cm – 8ins from shoulder seams. Join side and sleeve seams. Sew on front band and buttons. Press seams.

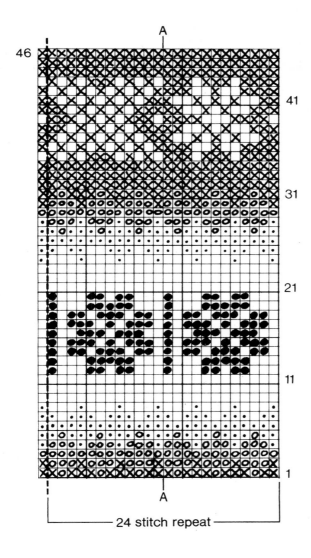

KEY

⊠	Dark brown
⊙	Mid brown
·	Light brown
□	White
⬤	Red

Faroe Island Sweater

A traditional Faroe Island design, with a seeded pattern main part and a diamond pattern yoke that follows the raglan shapings of the back, front and sleeves. The bold colour combination – red, white, green and blue – is typical of Faroe Island knitting. The borders are worked in two-colour striped rib.

The pattern is in three sizes, to fit 86cm (34 inch) to 97cm (38 inch) bust. Double knitting wool is used in the example shown. For a more traditional texture, Scottish Homespun or Shetland 3-ply, both double knitting equivalents, could be used. (See illustration page 36.)

Materials: Of Double Knitting Wool: 14 (15: 16) balls (25-gr) Red, 7 (8:8) balls White, 2 (2:2) balls each Green and Blue; two each 4mm (No 8) and 3¼mm (No 10) needles.

Measurements: To fit 86 (91:97)cm – 34 (36: 38)in bust; length, 66cm – 26ins; sleeve, 48cm – 19ins.

Tension: 11 sts and 12 rows to 5cm – 2ins over patt on 4mm (No 8) needles.

Abbreviations: See page 116.

Colour Abbreviations: R = Red; W = White.

Back

With 3¼mm (No 10) needles and R cast on 95 (101:107) sts. Work 2 rows in k1, p1 rib, beg 2nd row p1. Join W and work striped rib thus:
1st row: (right side). K1 R, (with W yfd, p1, ybk, with R k1) to end.
2nd row: P1 R, (with W ybk, k1, yfd, with R p1) to end.
These 2 rows form striped rib. Cont in striped rib until work measures 8cm – 3ins from beg, ending with a 2nd row and inc 1 st at end of last row*. 96 (102:108) sts.
Change to 4mm (No 8) needles and working in

st-st, beg k, work first 8 rows of chart until work measures 41cm – 16ins from beg, ending with a 4th or 8th row of chart.

Raglan Shaping: Work chart from row 9, casting off 1 (4:7) sts at beg of first 2 rows then dec 1 st each end of next and every following alternate row until 66th row of chart is completed. 38 (38:38) sts. Leave sts on spare needle.

Front

Work exactly as Back until 60th row of chart on Raglan Shaping is completed. 44 (44:44) sts.

Neck Shaping: *Next row:* K2 tog, patt 7, TURN. Work on these sts only. Shape raglan as before and dec 1 st at neck edge on every row until 1 st remains. Fasten off. Place centre 26 sts on a st holder. Complete other side of neck to match.

Sleeves

With 3¼mm (No 10) needles and R cast on 47 (53:53) sts. Work as Back to *. 48 (54:54) sts. Change to 4mm (No 8) needles and working in st-st, beg k, work first 8 rows of chart, inc 1 st end of every 5th row until there are 78 (84:90) sts, working extra sts into patt. Cont straight

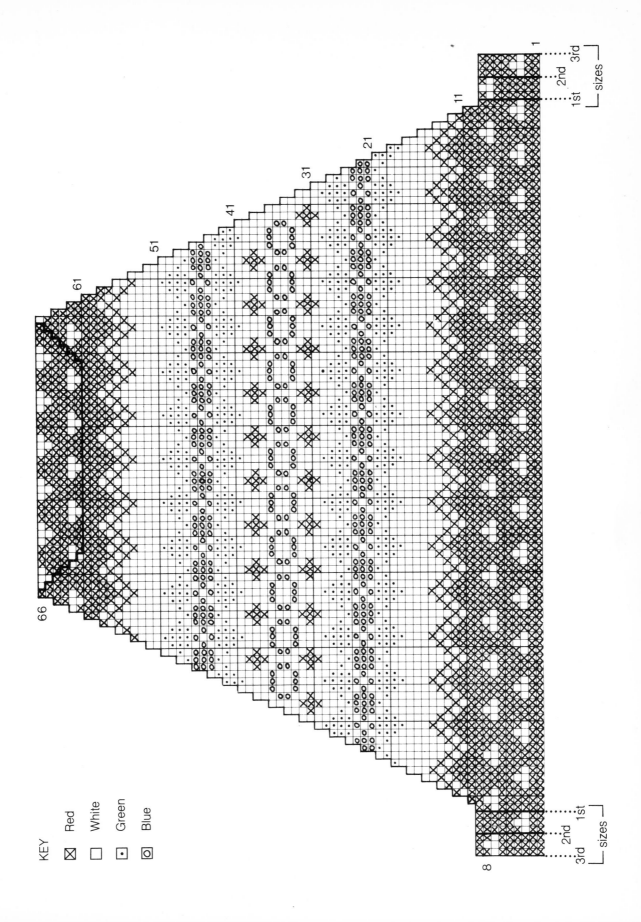

KEY

⊠ Red
☐ White
⊡ Green
◉ Blue

until work measures 48cm – 19ins from beg, ending with a 4th or 8th row of chart.

Raglan Shaping: Work exactly as Back, but with 18 sts less in overall chart patt and thus ending with 20 (20:20) sts after 66th row of chart instead of 38 (38:38). Leave sts on spare needle.

Neckband

Join both front and right back raglan seams. With 3¼mm (No 10) needles and R k sts of left sleeve, pick up and k 6 sts down left side of front neck, k sts from st holder, pick up and k 6 sts up right side of front neck then k sts from right sleeve and back neck. 116 sts.
Next row: P6, (p2 tog, p3) to end. 94 sts.

Work 2 rows in k1, p1 rib then work 6 rows in striped rib as Back. Cont in R only. Rib 2 rows more then cast off *loosely* ribwise.

Making up

Press lightly, omitting ribbing. Join left back raglan and neckband seam. Join side and sleeve seams. Press seams.

Faroe Island Waistcoat

A perfect example of Faroe Island knitting, with a seeded pattern main part and more intricate bands of pattern on the yoke only. Light beige is used for the background, with green, purple, blue and a small touch of brown for the contrast colours. The effect is equally striking if a dark background colour is used with light contrast colours. The front band can be reversed as it is worked separately and sewn on afterwards.

The pattern is in three sizes, to fit from 81cm (32 inch) to 107cm (42 inch) bust or chest. The waistcoat is knitted in Shetland 2-ply Jumper Weight wool, which is a 4-ply equivalent. (See illustration page 53.)

Materials: Of Shetland Wool 2-ply Jumper Weight (4-ply equivalent): 3 (4:4) hanks (2-oz) Light Beige (shade 202), 2 (2:2) hanks (1-oz) Green (47), 1 (1:1) hank (1-oz) each Purple (20), Royal Blue (18) and Ginger (45); two each 3mm (No 11) and 2¾mm (No 12) needles; 5 buttons.

Measurements: To fit 81–86 (91–97:102–107)cm – 32–34 (36–38:40–42)in bust or chest; length, 56 (60:63)cm – 22 (23½:25)ins.

Tension: 15 sts and 16 rows to 5cm – 2ins over patt on 3mm (No 11) needles.

Abbreviations: See page 116.

Colour Abbreviation: LB = Light Beige.

Back

With 2¾mm (No 12) needles and LB cast on 110 (120:130) sts. Work 8cm – 3ins in k1, p1 rib.
Next row: Rib 5 (inc in next st, rib 4) to end. 131 (143:155) sts.

Change to 3mm (No 11) needles and work 2 rows st-st, beg k. Still working in st-st, work first 10 rows of chart, ending k rows with first 5 sts of 6-st rep and beg p rows with last 5 sts, until work measures 33 (36:38)cm – 13 (14:15)ins from beg, ending with a 10th patt row.

Armhole Shaping: Now work from row 11 of chart, working left-hand side of work as mirror image of right-hand side BUT work centre stitch *once only*, and casting off 5 (7:9) sts at beg of next 2 rows then dec 1 st each end of next 6 (8:10) alternate rows as shown. 109 (113:117) sts. Cont from chart until row 82 (84:86) has been worked.

Shoulder Shaping: Work as chart and cast off 12 sts at beg of next 4 rows then cast off 12 (13:14) sts at beg of next 2 rows. Cast off remaining 37 (39:41) sts.

Left Front

With 2¾mm (No 12) needles and LB cast on 56 (61:66) sts. Work 8cm – 3ins in k1, p1 rib, beg 2nd row p1 *for 2nd size only*.
Next row: Rib 6, (inc in next st, rib 4) to end. 66 (72:78) sts.

Change to 3mm (No 11) needles and work 2 rows st-st, beg k. Now work first 10 rows of chart until work measures 33 (36:38)cm – 13 (14:15)ins from beg, ending with a 10th patt row.

Armhole and Front Shaping: Now work from row 11 of chart, shaping armhole as shown and *at same time* dec 1 st at front edge on next

113

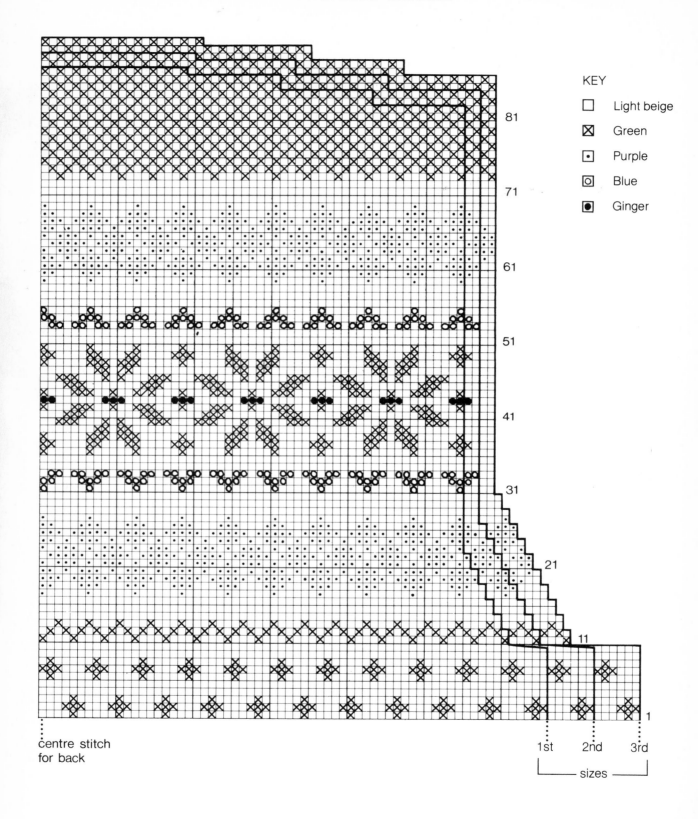

KEY

☐ Light beige

⊠ Green

· Purple

⊡ Blue

⬤ Ginger

centre stitch
for back

1st   2nd   3rd

sizes

and every following 3rd row until 36 (37:38) sts remain. Cont straight from chart until row 82 (84:86) has been worked.

Shoulder Shaping: Cast off 12 sts at beg of next and following alternate row. Work 1 row. Cast off.

Right Front

As Left Front but reverse shapings, i.e. cast off armhole sts at beg of row 12 of chart and shape shoulder after row 83 (85:87).

Front Band

Join shoulders. With $2\frac{3}{4}$mm (No 12) needles and LB cast on 8 (8:8) sts. Work 4 rows in k1, p1 rib.

Buttonhole row: Rib 3, cast off 2, rib 3.
Next row: Rib 3, cast on 2, rib 3.

Cont in rib, making 4 more buttonholes 7 (8: $8\frac{1}{2}$)cm – $2\frac{3}{4}$ ($3:3\frac{1}{4}$)ins apart (measure from base of previous buttonhole with work slightly stretched). Cont in rib after 5th buttonhole until band reaches up front, across back neck and down 2nd front, slightly stretched. Cast off.

Armbands

With $2\frac{3}{4}$mm (No 12) needles and LB pick up and k 130 (140:150) sts evenly around armhole edge. Work 8 rows in k1, p1 rib. Cast off ribwise. Work 2nd armband to match.

Making up

Press lightly, omitting rib. Join side and armband seams. Sew on front band, placing buttonholes to right front for a woman and to left front for a man. Press seams. Sew on buttons.

7
Abbreviations

k = knit
p = purl
st(s) = stitch(es)
st-st = stocking stitch
g-st = garter stitch
m-st = moss stitch
inc = increase
dec = decrease
tog = together
skpo = slip 1, knit 1, pass slip stitch over
tbl = through back of loop(s)
beg = beginning
rep = repeat
patt = pattern
cont = continue
alt = alternate
rem = remain(ing)
foll = following
yfd = yarn forward
ybk = yarn back

8
Suppliers

Guernseys (Chapter 4)

For the most part the traditional 5-ply Wool Worsted made especially for Guernseys is used in the patterns. We used Poppleton 5-ply, but Emu also make a Guernsey Wool 5-ply. Both firms are widely known but if you have trouble obtaining the wool, write to:

Richard Poppleton & Sons Ltd.,
Albert Mills,
Horbury,
Wakefield,
West Yorkshire WF4 5NJ

Emu Wools,
Leeds Road,
Greengates,
Bradford,
Yorkshire BD10 9TE

For Aran Wool and Shetland Wool see below.

Arans (Chapter 5)

Several large wool spinners produce 100% Wool Aran. We used Lister-Lee Aran for some of the designs but Emu and Sirdar also make a 100% Aran wool and all are made in a wide range of colours. Lister-Lee, Emu and Sirdar are all well distributed, but if you cannot find their Aran wool locally, write to:

Lister-Lee Wools,
PO Box 37,
Providence Mills,
Wakefield,
West Yorkshire WF2 9SF

Sirdar Ltd.,
PO Box 31,
Alverthorpe,
Wakefield,
West Yorkshire WF2 9ND

Emu Wools,
Leeds Road,
Greengates,
Bradford,
West Yorkshire BD10 9TE

For a slightly harder, Irish Aran wool, Blarney Bainin produced by Tivoli Spinners Ltd., Tivoli, Cork, is a suitable yarn.

Fair Isles, Shetlands and Faroes (Chapter 6)

The majority of the patterns are knitted in true Shetland wool or Fisherman's Scottish Home-spun Wool and both are available only by mail order. However, both firms provide a very good postal service.

For Shetland Wools:

Jamieson & Smith (Shetland Wool Brokers) Ltd.,
90 North Road,
Lerwick,
Shetland Isles ZE1 0PQ

For Scottish Homespun Wool:

A.N.I. Ltd.,
7 St Michael's Mansions,
Ship Street,
Oxford

Order information for the USA

When ordering any of the yarns used in this book, there will be a customs duty of $30 per 1lb of yarn *plus* 15 % of its value (1981).

We would suggest ordering the yarns directly from the companies listed on page 117, although Poppleton yarns can be obtained through:

Yarns from Afar,
4483 Nothmore Avenue,
Milwaukee,
Wisconsin 53211,
USA

The following suppliers in the USA are good sources of natural oiled yarns. All of them are equipped to handle mail orders.

Note: When knitting a pattern with yarn other than that specified in this book, it is *essential* to knit a tension square first since the yarn thickness may be completely different.

The Hook 'N' Needle,
1869 Post Road East,
Westport, Connecticut 06880
Telephone (203) 259-5119

Carries many brands of natural-oil, all-wool yarns.

Davidson's Old Mill Yarn,
PO Box 8,
109 Elizabeth Street,
Eaton Rapids, Michigan 48827
Telephone (517) 663-2711

Carries many brands of all-wool, custom-spun yarns. Sample card of natural-oil wools available for $2.00.

Phalice's Thread Web,
West 1301 14th Avenue
Spokane, Washington 99204
Telephone (509) 624-3423

Carries many brands of natural-oil, all-wool yarns.

The Wool Shop,
23 Monument Street,
Concord, Massachusetts 01742
Telephone (617) 369-4708/(617) 259-8588

Branch stores in Osterville and Wellesley, Massachusetts. Carries natural-oil yarns.

Yarn Depot,
545 Sutter Street,
San Francisco, California 94102
Telephone (415) 362-0501

Carries many brands of natural-oil, undyed yarns from Ireland and New Zealand.

Jan Knits,
Ingomar, Montana 59039
Telephone (406) 358-2267

Specialises in mail order business. Proprietors produce and sell their own yarn (including untreated black-sheep wool).

Joseph's Coat,
131 West Main Street
Missoula, Montana 59801
Telephone (406) 549-1419

Carries natural-oil, all-wool yarns.

9
Notes for American Readers

Needle conversion table

Current UK Metric Range	Former UK/Canadian Range	American Range
2mm	14	0
$2\frac{1}{4}$mm	13	1
$2\frac{3}{4}$mm	12	2
3mm	11	—
$3\frac{1}{4}$mm	10	3
$3\frac{3}{4}$mm	9	5
4mm	8	6
$4\frac{1}{2}$mm	7	7
5mm	6	8
$5\frac{1}{2}$mm	5	9
6mm	4	10
$6\frac{1}{2}$mm	3	$10\frac{1}{2}$
7mm	2	—
$7\frac{1}{2}$mm	1	—
8mm	0	11
9mm	00	13
10mm	000	15

Equivalent terms and abbreviations

English	American
needles	pins
tension	gauge
cast off	bind off
top shaping	cap shaping
work straight	work even
miss	skip
st-st (stocking stitch)	stockinette stitch
dc (double crochet)	single crochet
grafting	weaving

10
Bibliography

The Art of Knitting Eve Harlow (ed.), COLLINS, LONDON, 1977

The Craft of Knitting Rae Compton, STANLEY PAUL & CO., LONDON, 1976

Fisherman Knitting Michael Harvey and Rae Compton, SHIRE PUBLICATIONS, AYLESBURY, 1978

Patterns for Guernseys, Jerseys and Arans Gladys Thompson, DOVER, NEW YORK, 1971

The Sacred History of Knitting H. E. Kiewe, A.N.I., OXFORD, 1971

Textile Crafts Constance Howard (ed.), PITMAN, LONDON, 1978

Traditional Knitting Patterns James Norbury, DOVER NEW YORK, 1971